THE BOOK OF ICES

The 2022 Hardback Edition

Published by Morshead Publishing
27 Old Gloucester Street, London WC1N 3AX

www.morsheadpublishing.com

This supplemented hardback edition
copyright © 2022 Morshead Publishing

ISBN 978-1-913649-01-2

A catalogue record for this book is
available from the British Library and the
American Library of Congress.

Introduction to the 2022 Hardback Edition

GIVEN the constraints on female emancipation in the late Victorian era in which she commercially thrived, and even by today's standards, Agnes Bertha Marshall (*pictured*) was a remarkable achiever.

She was only in her 30s when *The Book of Ices* first appeared in the mid-1890s, yet she was already a respected chef and author who had previously published two general cookery books.

Even more impressive is that Agnes used her reputational and financial success to establish a cookery school in Mortimer Street, London (since rebuilt as an office block); publish a weekly subscription magazine; and launch an extensive range of Marshall-branded cookware, fruit and liqueur syrups, and general cookery ingredients. Many of them are adroitly specified in many of her recipes, though thankfully modern equivalents are available.

Agnes even ran an employment agency specialising in chefs, cooks, cook-housekeepers, butlers and other domestic staff.

Agnes Bertha Marshall was born in East London in 1855 but little is known about her early life, except that, following the untimely death of her father, she took an early professional interest in cookery, with *The Pall Mall Gazette* reporting that she "practised at Paris and with Vienna's celebrated chefs."

She married in 1878 but as an established chef, writer and entrepreneur she was understandably determined to retain her independence and to continue steering her various business interests, which she did until a horseriding accident in 1904 led to her death the following year.

We hope you will be entertained by and derive practical enjoyment and culinary pleasure from this new hardback edition of *The Book of Ices.* which presents all 118 of the original recipes for frozen desserts – including ice creams, mousses, sorbets, water ices, soufflés and accompaniments.

With the exception of several contemporaneous advertisements from the original edition presented again in this edition, the substantive text has been completely re-typeset slightly larger and in a sympathetic typeface to provide improved legibility. The illustrations have been digitally remastered to enhance the detail and charm of the original engravings. We have for authenticity retained period spellings (such as cocoanut, pine-apple and red currants) where they occur in the original collection.

This edition exclusively benefits also from a Glossary of cookery terms and ingredients, including equivalents to or substitutes for period or hard-to-find products; a guide to modern methods of making frozen desserts; and a reorganised and expanded Index that makes it easier to locate a particular recipe or key ingredient than did the original book.

Morshead Publishing have published also a new hardback edition of Agnes Bertha Marshall's complementary and more extensive 1894 work, *Fancy Ices* (ISBN 978-1-913649-00-5), which offers 343 original recipes and 86 period illustrations.

John Ransley

MORSHEAD PUBLISHING
LONDON, 2022

ESTABLISHED 1883

Telephone:

3115 }
6045 } MUSEUM.

Telegrams:

"MARSHALL'S COOKERY
WESTDO, LONDON."

MARSHALL'S
SCHOOL OF COOKERY

The oldest established, largest, and most successful
School of Cookery of its kind in the World. Specially
established for high-class French and English Cookery.

32-30, Mortimer St., London, W.1.

OFFICE HOURS 10 to 5   SATURDAYS 10 to 1

CLASS FEES.

(Payable in advance, or on admission)

Per day, Half Guinea.   6 days' course, £2.15s.

12 days' course, 5 guineas.   24 days' course, £9 guineas

Seven weeks' course, 35 lessons, 12 guineas.

Three months' course, 60 lessons, 20 guineas.

Fees are inclusive of all materials used, and pupils do practical work.

Pupils can join any day. Course Pupils need not attend consecutive days, but any time within two years.

* * *

CLASS HOURS.

Daily 11 a.m. till about 4 p.m. Saturdays excepted.

* * *

For Programme of Week, see "The Table" (page 81)

THE BOOK OF ICES

INCLUDING

CREAM AND WATER ICES,
SORBETS, MOUSSES, ICED SOUFFLÉS, AND
VARIOUS ICED DISHES,

WITH

NAMES IN FRENCH AND ENGLISH,

BY

A. B. MARSHALL.

(Copyright.)
REVISED AND ENLARGED EDITION.

London:

MARSHALL'S SCHOOL OF COOKERY, 32, MORTIMER STREET

PUBLISHED BY
ROBERT HAYES, LIMITED,
ROSEBERY HOUSE, BREAM'S BUILDINGS, E.C.4.

CONTENTS

24. Coffee (brown).
25 Coffee (white).
26. Cranberry.
27. Cucumber.
28. Curaçoa.
29. Damson.
30. Filbert.
31. Ginger.
32. Gooseberry.
33. Greengage.
34. Italian Cream.
35. Kirsch.
36. Lemon.
37. Marmalade.
38. Maraschino.
39. Neapolitan or Pinachée.
40. Noyeau.
41. Orange.
42. Orange Flower Water.

43. Peach.
44. Pear.
45. Pine-apple.
46. Pistachio.
47. Plum.
48. Quince.
49. Raspberry.
50. Ratafia.
51. Red Currant.
52. Rhubarb.
53. Rice.
54. Spanish Nut.
55. Strawberry.
56. Tangerine.
57. Tea.
58. Vanilla.
59. Walnut.
60. White Wine.

61. Made from Jams   62. Made from Fruit Syrups

63. Apple.
64. Apricot.
65. Banana.
66. Bergamot.

67. Black Currant.
68. Cedrat.
69. Cherry.
70. Cranberry.

CONTENTS

Sorbets, etc.   38

Mousses   42

Iced Soufflés   44

Dressed Ices, etc.   47

APPENDIX

SUPPLEMENT TO THE 2022 HARDBACK EDITION

THE BOOK OF ICES.

HINTS ON MAKING ICES.

1. Too much sugar will prevent the ice from freezing properly.

2. Too little sugar will cause the ice to freeze hard and rocky.

3. If the ices are to be moulded, freeze them in the freezer to the consistency of a thick batter before putting them in the moulds.

4. If they are to be served unmoulded, freeze them drier and firmer, so that the ices do not run.

5. Broken ice alone is not sufficient to freeze or mould the ices; rough ice and freezing salt must be used.

6. Fruit ices will require to be coloured according to the fruit. For Harmless Colours see p.76.

7. When dishing up ices, whether in a pile or moulded,

it will be found advantageous to dish them on a napkin or paper, as they will not conduct the heat to the bottom of the ices so quickly as the dish would.

Those who wish to be proficient can save themselves a great amount of time, trouble, and anxiety, as well as expense of materials, by attending at Marshall's School of Cookery on any day arranged for "Ices," when they will see the whole system in different branches practically taught, and be able to work from any recipes with ease.

FREEZING THE ICES.

Having prepared the cream, custard, or water ice as explained in the following recipes, take the Patent Freezer

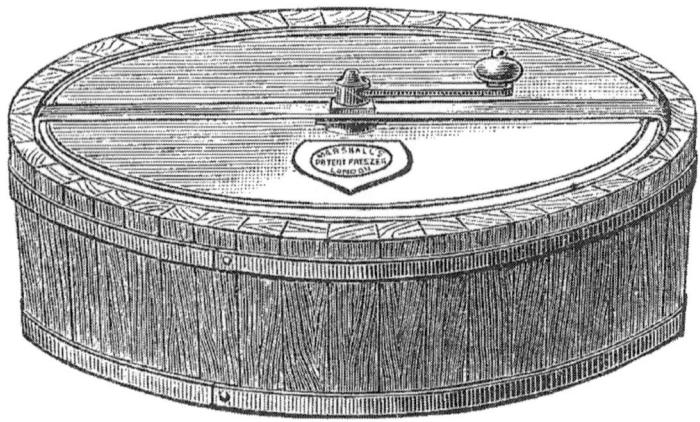

and lift the pan from the tub; put pounded ice in the tub to the depth of about 1 to inch, according to the quantity of cream, etc., to be frozen, and throw over the pounded ice half its weight of freezing or rough salt and mix it in with the pounded ice. Replace the pan on the pivot in the tub, leave

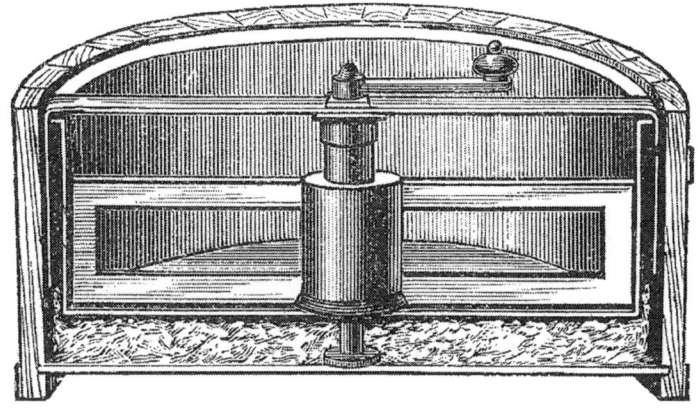

for 5 or 6 minutes to allow the freezer to become thoroughly cold, then pour your cream, etc., into the pan through the little door in the lid, and turn the handle. Observe, there is no need to pack ice and salt round the pan, but merely to put it on the bottom of the tub under the pan.

After turning the handle for 2 or 3 minutes, examine the progress of the freezing by looking through the door in the lid. When the cream is sufficiently frozen (see Hints 3 and 4, p.1), hold the pan with one hand and unscrew the handle and lift off the crossbar and lid.

Keep the freezer clean, and when cleaning take out the mixing fan.

N.B.—The cream, etc., in the pan should never be more than 1 inch deep. The shallower the layer is in the pan the quicker it will freeze.

For description, sizes, and prices of freezers, see p.70.

MOULDING AND KEEPING ICES.

Take a patent cave and remove the lids as shown in the annexed engraving, and fill in between the metals with a mixture of 2 parts broken ice and 1 part salt; shake it well down so that the mixture goes underneath the cupboard of the cave, and fill well up so that the lid will just slide over the ice and salt. Replace the lids and allow to stand for some 10-15 minutes before using.

Now fill your mould with the frozen cream from the freezer, and see that it is well pressed or shaken into the mould. Place the mould for 1½ to 3 hours in the cave; examine from time to time if you wish. When you desire to turn the ice out of the mould, dip the mould for an instant in cold water and turn it out as you would a jelly. If you put the ice, when turned out, back into the cave and shut the door, it will keep its shape for many hours, so that ices can he prepared long before actually required; they have thus been kept from one day to another. When anything is freezing in the cave, do not open the door more often than necessary.

When the cave is done with, remove the brine and wash out with boiling water, and see that it is put away dry.

For description, sizes, and prices of caves, see p.71.

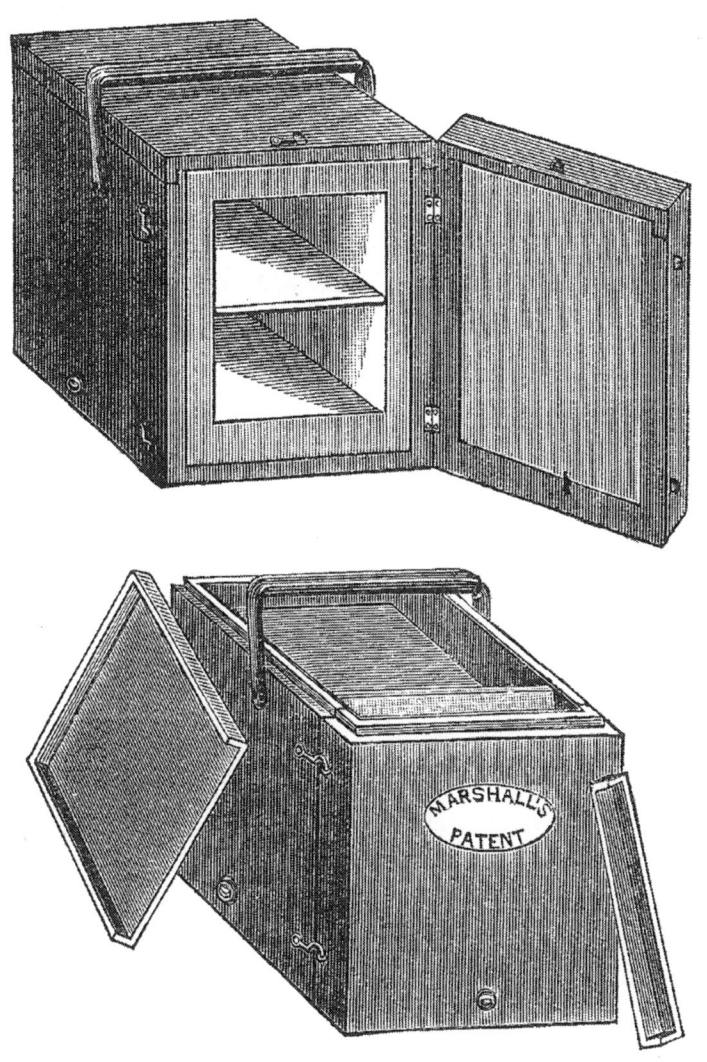

THE SACCHAROMETER.

This is an instrument for testing quantity of sugar in water ices, etc. To ensure uniform success, it is necessary that the strength of the syrups should always he the same. Instructions for using the instruments are sent with them (see p.76). Their use is strongly recommended.

ICE MOULDS AND MOULDING.

These are to be had in almost endless variety—a list of some popular ones will be found on pages 59-68.

In using ice moulds, great taste and novelty can be exercised in dishing up, and they afford to the cook the opportunity of making some of the prettiest dishes it is possible to send to the table.

CUSTARDS FOR CREAM ICES.

Never allow the *custard to boil*, or it will curdle.

Always add the flavouring when the custard is cooled, unless otherwise stated.

1.—Very Rich.

1 pint of cream, a quarter of a pound of castor sugar, and 8 yolks of eggs.

Put the cream in a pan over the fire, and let it come to the boil, and then pour it on to the sugar and yolks in a basin and mix well. Return it to the pan and keep it stirred over the fire till it thickens and clings well to the spoon, but do not let it boil; add 3 sheets of Marshall's gelatine, then pass it through a tammy, or hair sieve, or strainer. Let it cool; add vanilla or other flavour, and freeze. Mould if desired. When partly frozen, half a pint of whipped cream slightly sweetened may be added to each pint of custard.

2.—Ordinary.

Bring 1 pint of milk to the boil, then add 4 sheets of Marshall's gelatine, a quarter of a pound of castor sugar, and 8 yolks of eggs. Prepare this as in the above recipe. Flavour and freeze. This can be improved by using half a pint of milk and half a pint of cream instead of all milk.

3.—Common.

1 pint of milk, a quarter of a pound of sugar, and 2 whisked eggs. Put these in a pan and stir over the fire to *nearly* boiling. Remove it from the fire and stir in a quarter of an ounce of Marshall's gelatine (see p.77). When the gelatine is dissolved, pass it through the tammy, or hair sieve, or strainer. Flavour and freeze as above.

4.—Un-cooked.

Half a pint of new milk, ½ pint of cream or evaporated milk, 8 tablespoonfuls of any of Marshall's Fruit or Liqueur Syrup, colour according to flavour, add a few drops of lemon juice, and freeze. (No sugar is required.)

5.—PLAIN CREAM ICE *(Crème Glacée)*.

1 pint of cream sweetened with a quarter of a pound of castor sugar. Freeze dry.

This can be served in the centre of a compote of fruits, or with fresh fruits arranged round it; or the fruits and the cream can be served on separate dishes.

6.—CREAM ICES MADE FROM JAMS.

As jams vary exceedingly in the amount of sugar they contain, it is most necessary that this be taken into consideration to ensure success. The following recipe is for jams of average sweetness.

Boil 1 pint of milk and then mix it into 8 raw yolks of eggs, put this in a pan and stir over the fire until it thickens, then add 4 tablespoonfuls of jam, 4 sheets of Marshall's gelatine, and pass it through the tammy or hair sieve. When cool freeze, and when partly frozen add half a pint of whipped cream sweetened with half a teaspoonful of castor sugar. Colour the custard with a little red, green, yellow, or purple colour (p.76) according to fruit.

7.—Another way.

Take 4 tablespoonfuls of jam as above, and the strained juice of 1 lemon and 1 pint of cream; pass it through the tammy or hair sieve, and freeze it, Colour according to fruit.

8.—CREAM ICES MADE FROM FRUIT AND LIQUEUR SYRUPS

The syrups made by different manufacturers vary much in strength. The following recipe is for the syrups mentioned on p.75.

Make a custard as in Nos. 1, 2, 3, or 4, without sugar, and add 4 tablespoonfuls of syrup to half a pint of custard, and freeze. Mould or serve in a pile.

9.—Another way: very simple.

Add 4 tablespoonfuls of fruit purée or liqueur syrup to half a pint of cream or milk, and colour if necessary. Freeze. Mould or serve in a pile.

CREAM ICES MADE FROM RIPE FRUITS, ETC.

10.—Almond or Orgeat Cream Ice *(Crème d'Amandes*).*

Blanch, peel, and pound half a pound of sweet almonds mixed with 6 or 7 bitter ones. During the pounding add a teaspoonful of orange-flower water, 3 or 4 drops of essence of almonds, and a pint of tepid milk or cream (or half milk and half cream).

Sweeten with 4 ounces of castor sugar, and add to 1 pint of custard (Nos. 1 to 4) or 1 pint of sweetened cream (No. 5). Freeze and serve in a pile on a napkin, or mould it, or serve it in meringues or in little fancy papers. Serve as a dinner or dessert ice.

*The French names can be written in either of the following forms, as for Vanilla Cream Ice:—Crème à la Vanille, Crème de Vanille and the word "glacée" may be added; or Glace à la Vanille.

11.—Apple Cream Ice *(Crème de Pommes).*

Peel and cut up 2 pounds of good cooking apples, put them on the stove in ¾ of a pint of water, a little piece of cinnamon, the peel of a lemon, the juice of one, 2 bayleaves, 6 ounces of sugar, and 3 sheets of Marshall's gelatine. Cook quickly until reduced to a purée, then pass it through the tammy cloth or hair sieve, and mix it with 1 pint of sweetened cream (No. 5) or 1 pint of custard (Nos. 1 to 4). Add a few drops of Marshall's sap green. Freeze and serve as for previous recipe. Serve as a dinner or dessert ice.

12.—Apricot Cream Ice *(Crème d'Abricots).*

Cut 12 ripe apricots into halves, crack the stones, take out the kernels, and put the fruit to cook, for about a quarter of an hour, with 1½ pints of water and 4 ounces of loaf sugar. When tender mix a little liquid saffron or apricot yellow (p.76) with the fruit and a few drops of vanilla, and pass it through the tammy cloth or hair sieve.

Add this purée to 1J pints of custard (Nos. 1 to 4) or to the sweetened cream (No. 5). Freeze it, then add half a pint of whipped cream and a wineglass of kirsch syrup, and finish as for previous recipes.

Serve as a dinner or dessert ice.

13.—Banana Cream Ice *(Crème de Bananes).*

Peel 6 raw ripe bananas and pound them to a pulp, add the juice of 2 lemons, 2 oranges, and a glass of curaçoa (p.75). Pass it through the tammy cloth and finish with 1 pint of sweetened cream or custard as in previous recipe. Serve as a dinner, dessert, or supper ice.

14.—Biscuit Cream Ice *(Biscuits glacés à la Crème)*.

This ice can he made with the pieces of any kind of biscuit; rub them through the wire sieve and finish as for brown bread ice (No. 16). Serve as a dinner, dessert, or supper ice.

15.—Black Currant Cream Ice *(Crème de Cassis)*.

Put 1 pound of ripe black currants, 6 ounces of castor sugar, half a pint of water, the strained juice and peel of 2 lemons, and a few drops of carmine (p.76) in a pan, and let them just come to the boil. Pass it through the tammy and add 1 pint of custard (Nos. 1 to 4) or 1 pint of sweetened cream (No. 5), and 6 drops of lemon-juice. Partly freeze it, add half a pint of whipped cream, and finish as No. 10. Serve as a dessert ice.

16.—Brown Bread Ice *(Crème de Penn Bis)*.

Make a pint of brown bread crumbs and mix them with 8 tablespoonfuls of noyeau or maraschino syrup (p.75), a few drops of vanilla essence, and 1 pint of cream or unsweetened custard, and freeze dry. Serve in a pile or mould. This is a good entremet or dessert ice, and is much liked for garden and evening parties. It can also be served as a supper ice.

17.—Burnt Almond Cream Ice *(Crème de Pralines).*

Blanch and peel the almonds as in No. 10; put them in a saute pan with an ounce of fresh butter and an ounce of castor sugar, and fry till a dark brown colour. Then pound in the mortar till smooth, adding by degrees 1 pint of hot milk or cream, in which 4 sheets of Marshall's gelatine have been dissolved, sweetened with three ounces of sugar, and 3 or 4 drops of essence of almonds. Pass it through the tammy or hair sieve. Freeze and finish as in No. 10. Serve as a dinner or dessert ice.

18.—Cedrat Cream Ice *(Crème à la Cedrat).*

Take one or two cedratti and rub them well with four or five large lumps of sugar, then add these lumps with the strained juice to a quart of lemon cream ice, and freeze. Serve rough or mould. Serve as a dessert or supper ice.

19.—Cherry Cream Ice *(Crème de Cerises).*

Stone 1 pound of cherries, break the stones, take out the kernels, and cook the cherries and kernels for about 10 minutes in half a pint of water and 3 ounces of castor sugar; then pound them, add the juice of 1½ lemons, and a little carmine or cherry red to colour (p.76).

Pass it through a tammy cloth or hair sieve, add to a pint of custard (Nos. 1 to 4) or sweetened cream (No. 5) and a wine-glass of kirsch, and freeze. Serve in a pile on a napkin or mould it, and use as a dessert or supper ice.

20.—Chestnut Cream Ice *(Crème de Marrons)*.

Roast a quart of chestnuts, and when fully softened remove all husk and skin and pound them in a mortar, adding during the pounding by degrees a few drops of essence of vanilla, 3 ounces of castor sugar, a pint of tepid cream, and 6 drops of carmine (p.76). When well mixed pass it through hair sieve or tammy cloth.

This may be frozen as it is, or added to a pint of custard (Nos. 1 to 4) or sweetened cream (No. 5), and finished as in previous recipes. Serve as a dinner or dessert ice.

21.—Chocolate Cream Ice *(Crème de Chocolat)*.

Take a quarter of a pound of Fry's vanilla chocolate cut very fine, and put it in a stew pan with half a pint of milk or cold water on the stove to cook for about ten minutes; then add this to 1 pint of custard (Nos. 1 to 4) or 1 pint of sweetened cream (No. 5) and a few drops of vanilla essence. Freeze and finish as for vanilla cream ice (No. 58).

Cocoa cream ice may be made by adding 2 teaspoonfuls

of soluble cocoa to 1 pint of custard, and finished as usual.

22.—Cinnamon Cream Ice *(Crème de Gannelle)*.

Put 1 pint of milk or cream to boil with a finger- length of cinnamon, 1 bayleaf, and the peel of half a lemon; when well flavoured, add 4 sheets of Marshall's gelatine, and mix it on to 8 raw yolks of eggs and 4 ounces of castor sugar; thicken over the fire. Add a little apricot yellow (p.76); tammy, and finish as for other ices. Serve as a dessert ice.

22.—Cocoanut Cream Ice *(Crème de Noix de Coco)*.

Grate a small cocoanut, and stir this with 1 quart of custard or cream just as you take the latter from the fire. Strain it through tammy or hair sieve, flavouring it with a quarter-pint of rose or orange-flower water. Freeze it and mould as before. Serve as a dinner, dessert, or supper ice.

24.—Coffee Cream Ice *(Crème de Café)*.

Make 1 pint of strong coffee (or coffee extract is sometimes used), sweeten with 3 ounces of castor sugar; add this to 1 quart of custard (p.6). Freeze and finish as above. This ice will be brown, and not so delicate as the following. Serve as a dinner or dessert ice.

25.—White Coffee Cream Ice: very delicate
(Crème de Café Blanche).

Take a quarter of a pound of fresh roasted Mocha coffee berries, and add them to a pint of cream or milk in which dissolve 4 sheets of Marshall's gelatine; let them stand on the stove in a bain marie for an hour, but do not let them boil; sweeten with 3 ounces of sugar; strain through tammy. Freeze and finish as for vanilla cream ice (No. 58). Serve as a dinner or dessert ice.

26.—Cranberry Cream Ice *(Crème de Cranberges).*

Put 1 pound of cranberries in a pan with 6 ounces of castor sugar, a few drops of carmine (p.76), and half a pint of water. Cook until a pulp, then pass it through the tammy, add 1 pint of sweetened cream (No. 5) or custard (Nos. 1 to 4), and half a wine-glass of maraschino syrup. Freeze and finish as for previous ices, and serve for dessert.

27.—Cucumber Cream Ice *(Crème de Concombres).*

Peel and remove the seeds from the cucumber, and to 1 large-sized cucumber add 4 ounces of castor sugar, the peel of two lemons, and ¾ of a pint of water; cook till tender. Then pound and add to it a wineglass of ginger brandy, a little green colouring, and the juice of the two lemons; pass it through the tammy, and add to 1 pint of sweetened cream or custard.

Freeze and finish as usual, and serve for dessert.

28.—Curaçoa Cream Ice *(Crème au Curaçoa)*.

Take 1 pint of unsweetened custard (Nos. 1 to 4) or unsweetened cream; add the juice of 2 sweet oranges, 2 large wine-glasses of curaçoa or curaçoa syrup, 1½ ounces of castor sugar, a quarter-pint of orange-flower water and a few drops of vanilla essence. Freeze, and mould or serve roughly, for dinner or dessert ice.

29.—Damson Cream Ice *(Crème de Prunes de Damas)*.

Put 1 pound of ripe damsons to cook with 6 ounces of castor sugar, half a pint of water, the peel of two oranges, four bayleaves, and a little liquid carmine; just boil up and then pass it through the tammy; add the strained juice of the fruit. Add this to 1 pint of custard or cream (Nos. 1 to 5), and half a glass of noyeau syrup (p.75), and freeze. Serve as a dinner or dessert ice.

30.—Filbert Cream Ice *(Crème d'Avelines)*.

Shell and put 1 pint of filberts in a pan with cold water,

and put to boil; when they boil strain off and wash in cold water and rub them in a cloth to take off the skins. When this is done, put the filberts in the mortar and pound them till quite smooth; then mix with them gently 8 raw yolks of eggs, 1 pint of cream, 1 wine-glass of "Silver Rays" (white) rum, a wine-glass of noyeau syrup, and 4 ounces of castor sugar; put it into a pan and stir over the fire to thicken, keeping it stirred all the time; then pass through the tammy, add, when cold, a teaspoonful of essence of vanilla and ½ pint of whipped cream, and freeze. Serve as a dinner or dessert ice.

31.—Ginger Cream Ice *(Crème au Gingembre)*.

Pound half a pound of preserved ginger till smooth; then add to it 10 raw yolks of eggs, 3 ounces of sugar, 1½ pints of cream, and 1 glass of ginger wine; thicken it over the fire, then tammy or rub it through a hair sieve, and freeze. Serve as a dinner or dessert ice.

32.—Gooseberry Cream Ice
(Crème de Groseilles Vertes).

Put 1 quart of gooseberries on the stove in a pan, with half a pint of water, 6 ounces of castor sugar; boil, and when cooked pass through the tammy. If green berries, use a little sap green, or apple green (p.76), to colour; if red, a little carmine or cherry red. When tammied, mix with a pint of sweetened cream or custard, and freeze. Serve for dessert.

33.—Greengage Cream Ice
(*Crème de Prunes de Beine-Glaude*).

Stone 2 pints of ripe greengages, put half a pint of water in a pan with 8 ounces of castor sugar and 4 sheets of Marshall's gelatine, and boil the fruit in this till quite smooth; then add a little green colouring, a wine-glassful of maraschino syrup, and pass through the tammy. Add this to 2 pints of custard or cream (Nos. 1 to 5), and finish as usual.

34.—Italian Cream Ice (*Crème à l'Italienne*).

Scald 1½ pints of cream or milk, with a little lemon peel and cinnamon, and mix it on to 10 raw yolks of eggs, add 3 or 4 sheets of Marshall's gelatine; sweeten with 6 ounces of castor sugar; thicken over the fire, tammy, and flavour, when cool, with a large wine-glassful of pale brandy, half a glass of noyeau, the juice of 3 lemons, and a quarter-pint of rose-water. Freeze, and serve as in previous recipes, for dinner or dessert.

35.—Kirsch Cream Ice (*Crème au Kirsch*).

To 1½ pints of sweetened cream or custard add 3 wine-glasses of kirsch syrup, 1 glass of pale brandy, the juice of 3 oranges or lemons, and 3 or 4 drops of almond essence. Freeze. Serve as a dinner or dessert ice.

36.—Lemon Cream Ice *(Crème de Citron).*

Peel 6 lemons very thinly, and put this peel to boil, with 1½ pints of cream or milk and 5 ounces of sugar, for 10 minutes; add 3 or 4 sheets of Marshall's gelatine; then mix on to 10 raw yolks of eggs, thicken it over the fire and pass through the tammy. When cool add the juice from the lemons, which must be strained, and freeze. Serve as a dinner or dessert ice. Any peel left can be chopped up and used for flavouring puddings, cakes, etc.

37.—Marmalade, Orange or Lemon Cream Ice *(Crème au Marmelade).*

Mix 4 tablespoonfuls of marmalade with 1 pint of cream or unsweetened custard and the juice of 2 of the fruit, either lemon or orange, and 1 wine-glassful of orange or lemon syrup. Pass it through the tammy or hair sieve, and freeze. Serve as a dinner or dessert ice.

38.—Maraschino Cream Ice *(Crème au Marasquin).*
To I pint of cream or unsweetened custard add 4 wine-

glasses of maraschino or maraschino syrup and the strained juice of 2 lemons and I orange, and freeze. Serve for dinners or suppers.

39.—Neapolitan or Pinachée Cream Ices
(Petites Crèmes a la Napolitaine).

You must have a Neapolitan box for this ice (p.65), and fill it up in 3 or 4 layers with different coloured and flavoured ice creams (a water ice may be used with the custards); for instance, lemon, vanilla, chocolate, and pistachio. Freeze it in the patent ice cave for about to 3 hours, then dip the box into cold water for a second or two, turn out the ice, cut it into slices crosswise about ¼ inch thick, put each into a Neapolitan paper, and arrange neatly on a dish on a napkin or dish paper.

These ices can be arranged on a border of ice-water, when they should be prepared as follows: Take the oblong fancy border mould, fill it with cold water, put on the lid, and place it in the charged cave for 2 to 3 hours, then dip it into cold water, turn out the border on to a flat or dessert dish with a fancy paper, on which put a thin strip of wadding; arrange the Neapolitan ices in their papers on the border so that the various colours show up well; place on the ice a little sprig of maidenhair or asparagus fern; and use for a dinner or dessert ice, or for afternoon teas, tennis-parties, etc.

40.—Noyeau Cream Ice *(Crème au Noyeau)*.

To 1 pint of cream add 2 glasses of noyeau liqueur or 4 tablespoonfuls of noyeau syrup, and the juice of 2 oranges and 1 lemon. Freeze. Serve as a dinner or dessert ice.

41.—Orange Cream Ice *(Crème à l'Orange)*.

This is made as for lemon (No. 36), using oranges instead of lemons. Serve as a dinner or dessert ice. The peels can be chopped up and used for flavouring puddings, cakes, etc.

42.—Orange Flower Water Cream Ice *(Crème à la Fleur d'Oranger)*.

Blanch and skin 4 ounces of sweet almonds and 6 whole bitter almonds; pound them in the mortar till quite smooth, then mix with a quarter of a pint of cream, 6 ounces of castor sugar, and 7 raw yolks of eggs; add, when this is mixed well, 1¼ pints of cream, and then thicken over the fire, and then taminy.

When cool, add two wine-glasses of orange-flower water, a few drops of essence of vanilla, half a wineglass of "Silver Rays" (white) rum, and freeze it. Serve as a dinner, dessert, or ball supper ice.

43.—Peach Cream Ice *(Crème de Peches)*.

This is made in the same manner as the apricot ice. A *very* little carmine and apricot yellow is used for the colour. Serve for dinner or dessert.

44.—Pear Cream Ice *(Crème de Poires)*.

This is made in the same manner as the apple ice (No. 11), colouring with sap green or carmine, or it may be left plain. It can be served as a dinner or dessert ice.

45.—Pine-apple Cream Ice *(Crème d'Ananas)*.

Peel off the outside of the pine-apple; if not fully ripe, it will require to be boiled for about 20 minutes. Put the pine-apple in a clean pan with 1½ to 2 pints of water and half a pound of sugar, and cook till tender. Then pound, and pass through hair sieve or tammy.

To half a pint of this purée add 1 pint of cream or custard (Nos. 1 to 5). Freeze. Colour the ice required for the body of the pine-apple mould with apricot yellow, and that for the top with a little apple green. Another way is to make a purée of the tinned pine-apple, and add it to the custard or cream (Nos. 1 to 5). Serve as a dinner or dessert ice.

46.—Pistachio Cream Ice *(Crème de Pistachea)*.

Blanch, peel, and pound a quarter of a pound of pistachio kernels. Add, when thoroughly pounded, 2 tablespoonfuls of orange-flower water, and 12 drops vanilla essence; pass through sieve or tammy, and add 1 pint of sweetened cream or custard (Nos. 1 to 4).

Colour with apple green or sap green (p.76). Freeze and mould. Serve for a dinner or dessert ice.

47.—Plum Cream Ice *(Crème de Prunes)*.

Put 2 pounds of plums in a pan with half a pint of water, half a pound of castor sugar, a few drops of carmine, and the purée of 2 lemons; cook till smooth, and pass through the tammy. To half a pint of this purée add 1 pint of slightly sweetened cream or custard (Nos. 1 to 5). A few drops of essence of almonds and the strained juice of the lemons will improve it. Freeze and mould or serve in a pile, and use for a dinner or dessert ice.

48.—Quince Cream Ice *(Crème de Goings)*.

Take 4 tablespoonfuls of quince jam, and add to it the juice of 2 oranges and of half a lemon, 1½ pints of cream or custard (unsweetened), a little apricot yellow to colour,

2 tablespoonfuls of pine-apple syrup, a few drops of vanilla essence, and half a wine-glass of "Silver Rays" (white) rum. Pass it through the tammy and freeze it.

49.—Raspberry Cream Ice *(Crème de Framboises)*.

Take 1 pound of raspberries, 6 ounces of castor sugar, and the juice of a lemon; mix with one good pint of custard or cream (Nos. 1 to 5). Tammy, and colour with liquid carmine or cherry red (p.76). Freeze, and finish as for other ices. Serve as a dinner or dessert ice.

50.—Ratafia Cream Ice *(Crème au Ratafia)*.

Bruise 1 pound of ratafia biscuits in the mortar. Make a custard (see Nos. 1 to 4) of pints of milk, 10 raw yolks of eggs, and 6 ounces of castor sugar; and when it thickens, pour it over the bruised biscuits, and pass altogether through the tammy or hair sieve.

Add half a wine-glass of noyeau syrup, and freeze. The crumbs may be left in the custard if liked.

51.—Red Currant Cream Ice *(Crème de Groseilles)*.

Make this as for raspberry cream ice (No. 49), and serve for dessert, etc.

52.—Rhubarb Cream Ice *(Crème de Rhubarbe).*

Make this as for gooseberry cream ice (No. 32), using good ripe rhubarb; colour with Marshall's carmine, and use for suppers, tennis parties, etc.

53.—Rice Cream Ice *(Crème de Riz).*

Put 2 pints of new milk or cream to boil with 8 ounces of castor sugar, the peel of a lemon, 3 bayleaves, and a little crushed stick cinnamon, about 1 inch long; add 2 or 3 sheets of Marshall's gelatine, then put 3 ounces of rice cream *(crème de riz)* in a basin, and mix it into a smooth paste with cold milk, add the boiled milk, and let the whole simmer for 10 minutes. Pass it through the tammy, strainer, or sieve, and when cold add a few drops of essence of vanilla, and freeze. During the freezing add half a pint of slightly sweetened whipped cream that is slightly flavoured with vanilla essence. Mould or serve roughly, for dinner or dessert.

54.—Spanish Nut Cream Ice *(Crème de Noisettes).*

Break a pint of Spanish nuts and bake the kernels till crisp, then pound them till smooth, and add the raw yolks of 8 eggs, 5 ounces of castor sugar, and 1 pint of cream; put in a stew pan and stir over the fire till it thickens, then pass it through the tammy cloth. When cool, add a wine-glass of noyeau syrup, half a wine-glass of brandy, half a pint of stiffly whipped cream, and 2 stiffly whipped whites of eggs. Freeze and mould or serve in glasses, for a dinner or dessert ice.

Spanish Nut Cream Ice. Another way.

Put the kernels of a pint of Spanish nuts, with 2 ounces of castor sugar, the finely chopped peel of 2 oranges and a tablespoonful of orange-flower water, in a saute or stew pan, and toss over a quick fire until the kernels are quite brown; then pound in the mortar, and mix well with half a pint of cream. Pass through tammy cloth or hair sieve; flavour with 2 tablespoonfuls of maraschino or noyeau syrup (p.75). Add this to 1 pint of the sweetened custard or cream (Nos. 1 to 5) and 2 tablespoonfuls of sherry. Freeze and mould or serve rough, for dinner, etc.

55.—Strawberry Cream Ice *(Crème de Fraises)*.

Make this as raspberry cream (No. 49), and serve for a dinner ice.

56.—Tangarine Cream Ice *(Crème de Tangannes)*.

Peel 12 tangarine oranges; make a pulp of the insides,

first removing the pips. Put the peels in a pint of boiling cream or milk, and let it stand on the stove for a quarter of an hour, in a bain marie with boiling water round it, but do not let it boil; add 4 sheets of Marshall's gelatine, then mix this with 8 raw yolks of eggs and 4 ounces of sugar, and stir over the fire till it thickens; now add the orange pulp, colour with apricot yellow, and pass through the tammy or hair sieve; when cool, add a wine-glassful of orange flower water, and freeze. This may be added to 1 pint of sweetened cream or custard (Nos. 1 to 5) before freezing. Use for dinner, etc.

57.—Tea Cream Ice *(Crème de Thé).*

Prepare half a pint of very strong tea, sweetened with 2 ounces of castor sugar, and add this to 1 pint of sweetened custard or cream Nos. (1 to 5), and finish as for other ices. Use for teas, dessert, suppers, etc.

58.—-Vanilla Cream Ice *(Crème de Vanille).*

Prepare a custard (Nos. 1 to 4) or take sweetened cream (No. 5) and flavour with vanilla essence. Freeze and mould or serve in glasses, for ball suppers, dessert, etc. This is much improved by adding, during the freezing, a quarter of a pint of whipped cream to each pint of cream or custard.

To flavour with vanilla pods cut them in strips, and let

them boil with the milk or cream of your custard, keeping the pan covered. The pods can be used twice or thrice for flavouring milk, etc., and then, if they are pounded whilst quite dry with a little castor sugar and then rubbed through a hair sieve, the powder can be used for other purposes.

59.—Walnut Cream Ice *(Crème de Noix)*.

Make this as for filbert cream ice (No. 30), and Serve for dessert.

60.—White Wine Cream Ice *(Crème au Vin Blanc)*.

Prepare a custard (No. 1) with 10 raw yolks of eggs, 1 pint of cream, and 4 ounces of sugar. When cool, add 3 glasses of white wine, 1 ditto pine-apple syrup, and freeze. When frozen, mix in 6 ounces of finely cut preserved fruits of any kind you have, and mould if desired. Serve for dessert, etc.

FRUIT SYRUPS.

N.B.—If the prepared syrups referred to in some of the foregoing recipes cannot be got at the time required, recourse may be had to the syrup in recipe No. 87 for sweetening purposes.

WATER ICES.

61.—Water Ices made from Jams.

To 4 tablespoonfuls of jam add 1 pint of cold water, the juice of 1 lemon; colour according to the fruit; pass through the tammy, and freeze. See note to No. 6.

62.—Water Ices made from Fruit Syrups.

To half a pint of water add 4 tablespoonfuls of the syrup (p.75). Colour according to the fruit, and freeze. See note to No. 8.

WATER AND PERFUMED ICES MADE FROM RIPE FRUITS, ETC.

63.—Apple Water Ice *(Eau de Pommes)*.

Put 1 pound of apples to cook in a pint of water, with a little lemon-peel, cinnamon, the juice of 1 lemon and 4 ounces of sugar, add 4 sheets of Marshall's gelatine; when cooked, pass through the tammy, and add to 1 pint of the purée 1 pint of water sweetened with 4 ounces of sugar or 8 tablespoonfuls of syrup (No. 87). Freeze and serve moulded or roughly.

64.—Apricot Water Ice *(Eau d'Abricots)*.

Take 12 apricots and stone them, break the stones and pound the kernels; put the apricots to cook in a clean pan with 6 ounces of sugar, 1 pint of water, and cook them till quite smooth with 4 sheets of Marshall's gelatine; add a little apricot yellow, pass through the tammy, and add 1 pint of this pulp to 1 pint of water sweetened with sugar as in No. 63, or use the syrup No. 87, 8 tablespoonfuls to the pint of water, and freeze. Use for dessert, tennis parties, garden parties, etc.

65.—Banana Water Ice *(Eau de Bananes)*.

Peel 6 ripe bananas, pound them, and add 4 ounces of sugar, 1½ pints of water, and the juice of 2 oranges or a quarter-pint of orange-flower water, or lemons if preferred, a little banana essence if you have it; pass through tammy, and freeze. Serve for dessert, etc.

66.—Bergamot Water Ice *(Eau de Bergamote)*.

Prepare a lemon or orange water ice for this, and to 1½ pints of it add 2 wine-glasses of pale brandy and 6 drops of essence of bergamot. Freeze dry, and serve for dessert, suppers, etc.

67.—Black Currant Water Ice *(Eau de Cassis)*.

This is made in the same manner as the cranberry water ice, and can be used for tennis parties, dessert, etc.

68.—Cedrat Water Ice *(Eau de Cedrat)*.

Prepare 1 quart lemon water ice (No. 75), rub off the zest of two fine cedratti with a piece of loaf sugar, add to it the lemon water, tammy or strain it, and freeze. A quarter-pint of strained orange juice with 6 or 8 drops of vanilla essence is a great improvement. Serve for ball suppers or dessert.

69.—Cherry Water Ice *(Eau de Cerises)*.

Stone 2 pounds of Kentish cherries, crack the stones and pound the kernels, pour 1 quart of boiling water on the fruit and kernels and half a pound of sugar, add 4 sheets of Marshall's gelatine; colour with carmine and let stand till cold, then pass through the tammy, add a wine-glassful of kirsch, and, if liked, a wine-glassful of "Silver Rays" (white) rum or brandy, and freeze.

70.—Cranberry Water Ice *(Eau de Cranberges)*.

Put half a pound of cranberries to cook with 8 ounces

of sugar, the peel of 2 oranges and of 2 lemons, and half a pint of water; when cooked, add the juice of 2 lemons and 2 oranges, also dissolve in it 2 or 3 sheets of Marshall's gelatine, a little carmine, and pass through the tammy.

Add half a pint of this pulp to 1 pint of water slightly sweetened, and freeze.

71.—Damson Water Ice *(Eau de Prunes de Damas).*

Stone 1 quart of damsons and make in the same manner as cherry water ice (No. 69). Freeze either for fancy moulds or to serve rough.

72.—Ginger Water Ice *(Eau de Gingembre).*

Pound 8 ounces of preserved ginger, mix it with 1 quart of orange water ice (No. 79); pass it through the tammy, and freeze. Either mould or serve rough.

73.—Grape Water Ice *(Eau de Raisin).*

To 1 pint of lemon water ice (No. 75) add a large wine-glassful of elder-flower water and 2 wine-glassfuls of sherry, Freeze, and mould or serve rough. This will be greatly improved by the addition of a wineglass of "Silver Rays" rum.

74.—Jasmine Water Ice *(Eau de Jasmin).*

This is made in the same way as bergamot, only essence of jasmine is used instead of bergamot. Freeze for moulding or to serve rough. This is very good served with meringues arranged with whipped cream flavoured with vanilla and sweetened.

75.—Lemon Water Ice *(Eau de Citron).*

1 pint of boiling water poured on to the peel of 8 lemons, half a pound of loaf sugar, and 4 sheets of Marshall's gelatine; when cool, mix with the juice of 6 lemons; add 6 drops of lemon essence; tammy or strain through sieve, and freeze for moulding or for serving in glasses.

76.—Mille Fruits Water Ice *(Eau de Mille Fruits).*

Prepare 1 quart of lemon ice; add to it when partly frozen half a pound of mixed fruits cut in square pieces; any kind of fruit left from dessert will do for this ice. Serve in mould or rough.

77.—Melon Water Ice *(Eau de Melon).*

Take off the skin from a ripe melon about 1½ lbs. in

weight, and pound the melon till smooth, then add half a pint of boiling water in which 4 sheets of Marshall's gelatine has been dissolved, 3 ounces of sugar, the juice of 2 oranges or lemons, 1 wine-glass of curaçoa or maraschino syrup, 1 wine-glass of "Silver Rays" (white) rum, and ¾ ounce of ground ginger; add this to 1 pint of water, and freeze for moulding or to serve rough.

78.—Mulberry Water Ice *(Eau de Mûres)*.

Pick and then pound 1 pound of mulberries; add to them 4 ounces of sugar, a little liquid carmine, juice of 1 lemon; the addition of 2 wine-glasses of port is an improvement; pass through the tammy, then add to 1 pint of cold water, and freeze. Serve as in previous recipes for dessert, tennis parties, etc.

79.—Orange Water Ice *(Eau d' Oranges)*.

Prepare this the same as for lemon water ice, only use oranges instead of lemons, and serve for ball suppers, dessert, etc.

80.—Peach Water Ice *(Eau de Pêches)*.

Peel 6 good ripe peaches, crack the stones, and remove

the kernels, which must be pounded; put in a stew pan with 1 pint of water, 4 ounces of sugar, and juice and peel of 2 lemons; cook the fruit for 15 minutes, pound it up smoothly, then tammy, and add a wine-glassful of noyeau, 1 glass of orange flower water and the strained juice of two oranges, and a little carmine, Freeze, and use for ball suppers, dessert, etc.

81.—Pear Water Ice *(Eau de Poires)*.

Peel and core 6 good-sized mellow pears, cut them in slices, and put them to cook in 1½ pints of water with 6 ounces of sugar, the peel of 2 lemons, a pounded split vanilla pod 1 inch long, and a little cinnamon; add a little carmine and, when cooked, mix with a pint of lemon water ice; pass them through a tammy, and freeze.

82.—Pine-apple Water Ice *(Eau d'Ananas)*.

Peel the pine and take out the cores, put it to cook for 15 minutes, with 1½ pints of water, 6 ounces of sugar, and the juice of 2 lemons and 2 oranges, strain off the juice, pound the fruit; mix the liquor in which it was cooked with it and pass through the tammy or hair sieve, and freeze. A few pieces of the pine-apple may be cut in rounds or dice shapes, and added to the frozen ice just before serving. Mould if wished, and use for dessert, etc.

83.—Raspberry Water Ice *(Eau de Framboises).*

This is prepared the same as for strawberry water ice, only using raspberries instead of strawberries. Serve for dinners, suppers, etc.

84.—Red Currant Water Ice *(Eau de Groseilles).*

Proceed as for black currant water ice, only use red currants instead of black. Freeze, and mould if wished, and serve for dessert, ball suppers, tennis parties, etc.

85.—Rose Water Ice *(Eau de Roses).*

Take half a pound of fresh-gathered rose leaves, pour 1 pint of boiling water on them, with 4 ounces of sugar, and keep closely covered up; then strain off and colour with a little liquid carmine, ½ pint of rose water and a teaspoonful of vanilla essence, and freeze. Use for ball suppers, dessert, tennis parties, etc.

86.—Strawberry Water Ice *(Eau de Fraises).*

Put the strawberries in the mortar and pound them,

and to 1 pound add 6 ounces of castor sugar, the juice of 1 lemon, a little liquid carmine; pass though the tammy or hair sieve, mix this to 1 pint of cold water, and freeze. Serve as in previous recipes for ball suppers, dessert, tennis-parties, etc.

87.—Syrup for Water Ices.

Put 1½ pounds of loaf sugar in a clean pan to boil with 3 pints of cold water, keep well skimmed, reduce to half the quantity, and strain through the tammy or clean cloth. This will keep well. It may be used for sweetening the ices instead of the sugar, and if 4 sheets of Marshall's gelatine are dissolved in each pint of the water, it greatly improves the ice-making, and creates a much smoother creamy ice.

SORBETS, ETC.

THE Italian word *sorbetto*, meaning sherbet, shows the origin of these dishes. Their general character is that of a water ice mixed or flavoured with wine or spirits. They are served before the roast in glasses or fancy cups, and generally just enough frozen to be piled up in the glass, or they may be moulded in little shapes and served with or without fruit. The following recipes will be sufficient for guidance, and they can be varied according to desire.

88.—Sorbet of Peaches
(Sorbet de Pêches à la Portugaise).

Take 6 ripe peaches, peel them, and add to them 6 ounces of castor sugar, the juice of 2 oranges or 1 dozen grapes; crack the stones, pound the kernels and put to the fruit, and add to 1 pint of cold water, in which 4 sheets of Marshall's gelatine has been dissolved; add about 6 drops of Marshall's carmine and half a saltspoonful of apricot yellow, and tammy; then freeze.

When frozen add 1 wine-glassful of kirsch, a wine-glass of "Silver Rays" (white) rum, and serve with sliced fresh peaches that have been sprinkled with any nice liqueur and then left on ice till quite cold but not frozen, and chopped pistachio nuts over, for dinner, dessert, tennis, etc.

89.—Sorbet of Strawberries *(Sorbet de Fraises).*

Take 1 pound of strawberries, and add to them 8 ounces of castor sugar, a little carmine, and the juice of 1 lemon; pass through the tammy, and to this add 1 pint of water, in which 3 or 4 sheets of Marshall's gelatine has been dissolved, and partly freeze; then add 1 wine-glassful of curaçoa (p.75), half a wine-glassful of "Silver Rays" rum; continue the freezing, and serve in sorbet cups or glasses.

If you have little strawberry moulds, you can put the

sorbet in them, and freeze them for about half an hour in the cave. Serve with cut fresh fruits over, which have been flavoured by being tossed in a little brandy and castor sugar.

90.—Sorbet of Apricots
(Sorbet d'Abricots à la Moscovite).

Take 4 tablespoonfuls of apricot jam, about a salt-spoonful of apricot yellow, 1 pint of cold water, pass through the tammy and freeze; then add 1 wine-glassful of maraschino (p.75) and half a wine-glassful of "Silver Rays" rum; freeze firm, and serve on a dish on a paper or napkin with square pieces of apricots, cherries, and angelica that have been sprinkled over with a little maraschino syrup. In summer-time fresh fruit can be used, when the fruit should be cut up and a little sugar sprinkled over it before serving. This is served in sorbet cups or glasses or in a coupe shape.

91.—Roman Punch *(Punch à la Romaine).*

Boil 1 quart of water, and add to it 1 pound of sugar; when quite boiling, pour it on to the peel of 6 lemons, add ¼ ounce of Marshall's gelatine, cover it over till cold, then add the juice of 6 lemons; strain it through the tammy, and freeze; when partly frozen, add 2 wine-glasses of "Silver Rays" (white) rum, and serve in sorbet cups or in glasses, or in a coupe shape, standing it on a serviette, for dinner, ball supper, etc.

92.—Another way.

Make 1 quart of lemon water ice in which ¼ ounce of Marshall's gelatine has been dissolved; when cold, have the whites of 5 eggs whipped stiff, with a tiny pinch of salt, then mixed with 4 ounces of castor sugar; partly freeze the lemon ice, and then mix to it the whipped egg, and continue freezing in the machine till smooth; when smooth, add 1 large wine-glassful of brandy and a half-pint of champagne; freeze it to the proper consistency, and serve in sorbet cups or glasses, or in a coupe shape, and serve for dinner, ball supper, etc.

93.—American Sorbet *(Sorbet à l'Americaine)*.

Make some imitation glasses, by freezing water in the proper tin moulds prepared for the purpose, and make a sorbet as above, flavouring it with Catawba wine or champagne. Serve the sorbet in the imitation glasses. These imitation cups or glasses can be made transparent, marble-like, or coloured. Use for any cold collation or for dinner.

94.—Rum Sorbet *(Sorbet au Rhum)*.

Prepare a lemon water ice, and when nearly frozen,

flavour with 2 wine-glasses of "Silver Rays" rum to the pint of prepared ice, refreeze it to proper consistency and serve for dinner or any cold service.

MOUSSES.

THESE make excellent sweets, and are very much liked on account of their lightness. They are served as an entremet, sometimes for dessert. The following recipes will show the method of making them.

Mousses are greatly improved in appearance if, after they are turned out of the moulds, they are replaced in the charged ice cave, on a little tray or dish, and allowed to remain for 20 to 30 minutes before being used.

95.—Coffee Mousse (*Mousse au Café*).

Put into a stew pan 4 raw yolks of eggs, 2 whites, 1 ounce of castor sugar, 1 large tablespoonful of strong coffee, or 4 tablespoonful of coffee essence, and A saltspoonful of vanilla essence; whip over boiling water or over a fire till it is warm, then take off and whip till cold and like a stiff batter, and then add half a pint of stiffly whipped and slightly sweetened cream; mix these together, being careful not to overstir, after the cream is added, or it will be liable to curdle. Put in a plain bomb or other mould, and place in the charged ice cave to freeze for about 3½ hours. To turn out, dip the mould in cold water, pass a clean cloth over the bottom to absorb any moisture. Serve with dish-paper, or napkin on dish, for dinner or dessert.

96.—Strawberry Mousse *(Mousse aux Fraises)*.

Put 4 raw yolks of eggs into a pan, with 2 whites of eggs, 2 ounces of castor sugar, a quarter of a pint of the pulp of fresh strawberries, 1 teaspoonful of essence of vanilla, a little of liquid carmine to colour; whip till warm over boiling water, as in previous recipe, then remove and whip till cold and thick, and add half a pint of lightly sweetened whipped cream; mix carefully together, put into any fancy mould, and freeze for about 3½ to 4 hours in the cave. Turn out and dish same as No. 95. When fresh fruits are not obtainable, 2 tablespoonfuls of strawberry syrup with a few drops of lemon juice can be used instead.

97.—Maraschino Mousse *(Mousse au Marasquin)*.

This is made in the same manner as the Mousse a la Vanille, but instead of the vanilla essence add 1 good wine-glassful of maraschino for flavour, and use for dinner or dessert.

98.—Vanilla Mousse *(Mousse à la Vanille)*.

Put 6 yolks of eggs into a whipping-pan, with 2 whites, 1 ounce of castor sugar, half a tablespoonful of essence of vanilla, and a tablespoonful of brandy; whip this over boiling water till warm, then remove the pan from the fire and continue whipping till cold and thick, then add to this half a pint of slightly sweetened whipped cream; put into any kind of mould, and set in the ice cave for to 4 hours. Turn out same as No. 95.

ICED SOUFFLÉS.

THESE very much resemble the Mousses, but as they are served in dishes or cases, and the mousses are moulded. A slight difference is required in the ingredients and in the time for freezing. The following recipes will be sufficient for guidance.

99.—Coffee Soufflé *(Soufflé au Café)*.

Take a soufflé dish or paper soufflé case and surround it outside with paper standing about 2 to 3 inches above the top, and if a dish is used put it into the charged cave to get cold.

Put into a whipping tin and whip over boiling water 2 raw yolks of eggs, 2 whole, 1 large tablespoonful of very strong coffee, 1 ounce of castor sugar, until like a thick batter, then remove and continue the whipping till the mixture is cold; to this quantity add ¼ pint of slightly sweetened whipped cream; pour this into the case, letting it rise above the case to near the top of the paper. Freeze in the cave for 3½ to 4 hours, and serve in the case with a folded napkin round or a fancy paper band; place the soufflé on a flat dish on a paper, and serve for dinner or dessert. Of course these quantities may be proportionately increased or diminished to suit the size of the dish or case.

100.—Vanilla Soufflé *(Soufflé à la Vanille).*

Prepare the soufflé dish or paper case as in No. 99. Put into a whipping-tin 4 raw yolks of eggs, 2 whites, 1 ounce of castor sugar, a saltspoonful of vanilla essence, and a dessert-spoonful of brandy; whip over boiling water until warm, then remove it and whip it cold and like a thick batter; then add about pint of lightly sweetened whipped cream. Finish as in No. 99, and serve for dinner or dessert.

101.—Strawberry Soufflé *(Soufflé de Fraises).*

Prepare a mousse as in No. 96, using about half as much

more cream whipped, finish as in last recipe, and serve for dinner or dessert.

102.—Coffee Soufflés in Cases
(Petits Soufflés au Café).

Take the little paper soufflé cases and fasten round the outside of each a strip of white foolscap paper, about 3 inches deep, fixing it with sealing wax; let the paper stand about 1½ inches above the top of the case. Prepare some of the soufflé mixture as in No. 99; fill the cases to nearly the edge of the paper surrounding them, and place them in the charged cave for 2½ to 3 hours; when frozen sufficiently remove the papers and slip each case into a little fancy paper case, and serve on a flat dish on a fancy paper, for dinner, or dessert, or any cold collation.

Any soufflé can be served in a similar manner. Fruit and vanilla soufflés would be improved in appearance by sprinkling a little coloured sugar over them, or a little finely chopped pistachio. They are also pretty when garnished on the top with a little rose shape of sweetened, flavoured, and mottled cream, forced through a forcing-bag and large rose pipe. They may also be garnished with raw or ripe fruits which have been glazed with boiled sugar.

DRESSED ICES, ETC.

Iᴛ is impossible to give more than a few under this head, as the variety that can be made with the various moulds, flavours, etc., is almost unlimited; but the mixtures which can be used will be found among the foregoing recipes, and some designs in colours are given in the book as examples, also a list of some moulds on pages 59 to 68.

103.— Strawberry and Vanilla Bombe
(Bombe à la Vanille et Fraises).

Prepare 1 pint of strawberry water ice and freeze it quite dry, have three-quarters of a pint of vanilla custard prepared with three-quarters of a pint of milk or cream boiled with a stick of vanilla pod, 2 ounces of castor sugar, 2 sheets of Marshall's gelatine, and when flavoured sufficiently pour on to 4 raw yolks of eggs and thicken over the fire; then tammy and freeze, and add, when partly frozen, 3 tablespoonfuls of maraschino syrup and 6 drops of brandy; line a bombe mould with the strawberry water ice, and fill up the centre with the vanilla custard, and freeze for 3½ to 4 hours in the charged patent ice cave. To turn out, dip the mould in cold water, pass a clean cloth over the bottom to absorb any moisture, and serve on a napkin or fancy paper on a flat dish or plate, for a dinner ice.

104.—Bombe with Fruits *(Bombe aux Fruits).*

Take a bombe mould, which should be stood in a basin or tin with a mixture of ice and salt all round it, and line it with chocolate ice cream, then fill up the centre with vanilla cream ice mixed with a wine-glassful of kirsch, half a pint of whipped cream, and a quarter of a pound of candied fruits cut in small dice pieces which have been soaked in a tablespoonful of noyeau syrup. Freeze in charged ice cave for 4 hours, turn out as in last recipe, and serve on a dish- paper or napkin.

105.—Sovereign Bombe *(Bombe à la Souveraine).*

Line the sides and top of a bomb-shaped mould with a layer of almond ice cream, and fill up the interior with a tea mousse (see recipe No. 95 for coffee mousse).

Freeze in the cave for 3 to 4 hours according to size of mould; when ready to use turn out the ice in the usual way, and serve it on a border of sponge cake, and garnish the dish with the same cake cut in small fancy shapes.

106.—Plain Ice Pudding *(Ponding Glacé).*
To 1½ pints of good cream add half a pint of new milk;

put it in a stew pan with the raw yolks of 12 eggs, a pinch of mixed spice, half a pound of castor sugar, 1 split pod of vanilla; stir this over the fire till it thickens and presents a creamy appearance on the wooden spoon, then add 4 sheets of Marshall's gelatine; tammy it.

When cool add a large wine-glassful of brandy or "Silver Rays" rum, a wine-glassful of kirsch, 4 ounces of dried mixed fruits cut up into dice shapes, and half a pint of slightly sweetened whipped cream; freeze, and put into any mould and freeze in the cave for 2 hours. Serve for dinner or dessert.

107.—Nesselrode Pudding *(Ponding à la Nesselrode)*.

This is prepared the same as No. 106, with the addition of various cut fruits, and 1 ounce of shelled blanched Jordan almonds cut into dice shapes and baked brown, being mixed with the custard before putting into the mould. If fresh or dried fruits are used, they should be soaked in a little liqueur or spirit and sprinkled with sugar before being mixed. Fruits preserved in syrups may simply be cut up and mixed.

108.—Sauce for above.

A sauce is sometimes served with the Nesselrode pudding, and is made by preparing a thick rich custard (No. 1) and flavouring it with vanilla or maraschino. Keep it on the ice, and serve as cold as possible.

109.—Chateaubriand Bombe
(Bombe à la Chateaubriand).

Prepare 2 pints of vanilla custard (Nos. 1 to 4), put the milk to boil with 4½ ounces of castor sugar and 1 pod of vanilla split in shreds; let this come to the boil, and remain on the side of the stove in a bain marie pan covered up for about 15 minutes, but it must not boil; add 4 sheets of Marshall's gelatine, then mix it on to 12 raw yolks of eggs and thicken over the fire. Divide the custard into two parts; put to one part a few drops of essence of vanilla and ¼ pint of orange-flower water, and colour it with apple green to the colour of pistachio, and tammy; it is ready then to freeze, but when partly frozen put about ½ pint of whipped cream, sweetened with half a teaspoonful of castor sugar.

Put 3 ounces of blanched sweet almonds in a saute pan, with half an ounce of fresh butter and 1 ounce of castor sugar; make these quite a deep brown over the fire, and then pound them quickly in the mortar till smooth; mix them with the other part of vanilla custard, and pass through the tammy; when frozen, add cream as to the other part of the custard, and freeze.

Arrange the two ices thus prepared in a fancy mould in

layers, or the mould can be entirely lined with the green, and the centre filled with the brown ice. Freeze for 2 hours in the cave, and serve for a dinner or dessert ice.

110.—Ginger Bombe *(Bombe au Gingembre).*

Prepare a custard made with a pint of milk, boiled with the peel of 2 lemons and 3 ounces of castor sugar; when the milk boils, mix it on to 4 raw yolks of eggs and as much ginger as will cover a threepenny piece, thicken over the fire and tammy, then add the strained juice of the lemons and 6 drops of vanilla essence, and when cool freeze; when partly frozen, add half a pint of whipped cream sweetened with half an ounce of castor sugar. Line the bombe mould with this, forming a well, and have 3 ounces of preserved ginger cut in dice shapes and flavoured with a little maraschino and put in the centre; fill up with more of the custard, and freeze for 3½ hours in the cave. Turn out in the usual way and serve on a napkin or dish-paper, for dinner or dessert.

111.—Bartlett Pudding *(Pouding à la Bartlett).*

Peel and cut up in thin slices 6 ripe Bartlett pears, cook them in 1½ pints of water with the juice of 2 lemons, 6 ounces of sugar; when tender, add 3 or 4 sheets of Marshall's gelatine, drain them on a sieve, and pass the fruit through a tammy or fine hair sieve; mix with this 2 ounces of pine-apple cut fine, 2 ounces of dried cherries, and a pint of thick cream, and freeze; when partly frozen, have ready to mix with it the whipped whites of 3 eggs, to which have been added 2 ounces of sugar, cooked to caramel. For this, put the sugar to boil with a quarter of a pint of water, and when cooked add 2 ounces more of water, and when boiled up and liquid mix it with the eggs and add to the frozen mixture, and continue the freezing, and mould. Put it to freeze in the charged ice cave for 3½ to 4 hours, then turn out as usual. A little of the syrup from the pears must be used for the sauce for serving round the pudding. Prepare it as follows: Whip the white of 1 egg and mix it with 2 tablespoonfuls of whipped cream, half a wine-glass of maraschino syrup (p.75); add a wine-glassful of the pear syrup and cool on ice. When the pudding is turned out, pour the sauce over it, and serve for a dinner sweet.

112.—Plombière of Strawberries
(Plombière de Fraises).

Put 1 pint of thick cream in a pan with the raw yolks of 12 eggs, a tiny pinch of mixed spice, and half a pound of castor sugar; stir together on the stove, and when nearly boiling add to it 4 sheets of Marshall's gelatine, 1 pint of the pulp of fresh strawberries which has been passed through the tammy cloth, a little carmine, half a teaspoonful of essence of vanilla, a wine-glass of brandy, 3 whipped whites of eggs, and half a pint of whipped cream; freeze and mould, and leave in the ice cave for 4 hours; then dip in cold water, and turn out on to a napkin or dish-paper.

113.—Muscovite of Oranges *(Moscovite d'Oranges).*

Put half a pound of loaf sugar with the peel of 8 or 10 oranges, a quarter of an ounce of Marshall's gelatine, and pour over them 1 pint of boiling water and a little saffron yellow; let this stand till cool, then mix the juice of the oranges to it and strain through the tammy, add a wine-glass of maraschino and brandy to flavour. Pour into a mould and freeze for about 4 hours in the charged ice cave; turn out as in the last recipe. This can be served with whipped cream sweetened and flavoured, which should be arranged in the form of a rose by means of a forcing-bag and large rose pipe, and also with a compote of oranges or other fruits, either fresh or preserved, flavoured with any nice liqueur. Use for a sweet for dinner, etc.

114.—Muscovite of Strawberries
(Moscovite de Fraises).

Pass 1 pound of ripe strawberries through the tammy, add 6 ounces of castor sugar, 1 pint of warm water, in which has been dissolved a quarter of an ounce of Marshall's leaf gelatine, the juice of 1 lemon, a little carmine, and a little noyeau; pour into a mould, and put to freeze for about 3 hours in the cave. To turn it out, put the mould into cold water for a few seconds. This can be served with cream or fresh strawberries, mixed with a little syrup, coloured with a few drops of Marshall's carmine, for a dinner or luncheon sweet or for a ball supper.

115.—Little Soufflés of Cheese
(Petits Soufflés de Fromage Glaces).

Put into a clean pan 3 ounces of finely grated Parmesan cheese, 2 ounces of gruyère cheese, a good pinch of salt, a dust of Marshall's Coralline pepper, and a dust of castor sugar; mix with these ingredients half a pint of strong aspic jelly, that has been taken when cooling and whipped till spongy but not set, then stir into it three-quarters of a pint of stiffly whipped cream and a dessertspoonful of Marshall's white tarragon vinegar.

Stir quickly together, put into a large forcing-bag with a large plain pipe and three-parts fill up some little paper or china cases, that have been surrounded with little narrow strips of foolscap paper cut about 2½ inches wide and 7 or 8 inches long, and fastened tightly round the cases with sealing-wax.

Place the cases on the shelf of the charged ice cave for about three-quarters of an hour, then when about to use remove the paper bands, sprinkle over the tops of the soufflés a few browned bread-crumbs, place on the top of each soufflé a little sprig of crisp fresh watercress or any other pretty little light salad, or scalloped cucumber or radish; dish them up on a dish-paper, and use for a second-course dish, or for savoury, or for a ball supper, etc.

116.—Iced Spinach à la Crème
(Epinards Glades à la Crème).

Put 2 or 3 handfuls of well-washed spinach in cold water with salt, and a very tiny pinch of bicarbonate of soda; let it come to the boil; strain off and press the water from it. Boil half a pint of milk and stir it on to 4 raw yolks of eggs, and put it on the stove again to thicken—don't let it boil; add a little of Marshall's sap or apple green to colour it if needed, and to half a pint of the custard add a small dessertspoonful of castor sugar and a pinch of salt; mix with the spinach.

Pass through the tammy, and freeze; add, when partly frozen, a teacupful of whipped cream sweetened with a very slight dust of castor sugar. Freeze dry and mould in a Neapolitan box in the charged cave for about hours; then cut it crosswise into slices about a quarter inch thick, and stamp them out with a cutter into cutlet shapes.

Prepare an iced cream as follows : Take 1 pint of cream, 1 tablespoonful of castor sugar, 1 tablespoonful of orange-flower water, and a few drops of vanilla. Freeze it dry and mould some of it in a plain border mould, leaving the remainder for garnishing.

When the border is frozen, turn it out in the usual way on to an entrée dish on a paper; place the cutlets en couronne on the border, fill up the centre with the remainder of the frozen cream, place a little asparagus or maidenhair fern over, and, if liked, a little cutlet frill may be placed in the top of each cutlet. Use. for second course or for ball suppers, etc.

117.—Soufflés of Curry à la Ripon
(Petits Soufflés de Kari à la Ripon).

Fry in a clean stew pan about 2 ounces of fresh butter, 2 onions sliced, 2 sour apples, a sprig of thyme, 2 bayleaves, sprig of parsley, about 1 ounce of freshly grated cocoanut and 6 almonds blanched and pounded; to this add a raw or cooked sole or whiting.

Fry all until a good golden colour, then add half a teaspoonful of Marshall's curry powder, half a teaspoonful of curry paste, half a teaspoonful of tamarind pulp, a little salt, coralline pepper, and a tablespoonful of Marshall's (white) tarragon vinegar; cover then with 1 pint of milk and cook till tender.

Add a little saffron yellow (page 76) to colour, and 3 sheets of Marshall's gelatine.

Take the meat from the fish-bone and pound it, and pass all the ingredients through a tammy cloth; add a quarter of a pint of this purée to a good quarter of a pint of whipped aspic and half a pint of whipped cream; stir up well together, pour it into little cases that have been surrounded with little bands of white foolscap paper in the usual way.

Set them in the charged ice cave for about 1 hour, then when ready to serve, remove the bands of paper, sprinkle the soufflés with finely chopped raw parsley and a little finely chopped aspic jelly, dish up on a dish-paper and use for an entrée for dinner, etc.

Aspic Jelly for No. 117.

Two and a half ounces of Marshall's gelatine, one quart of water, a dessertspoonful of salt, juice of one lemon, one or two bayleaves, two whites and shells of eggs, a small teacupful of Marshall's (white) tarragon vinegar, one onion sliced, and twenty peppercorns and allspice mixed.

Mix up all the ingredients well with a whisk, and when it comes to the boil, pass it through a warm jelly-bag, having first run some boiling water through the bag.

This is made stiff for borders; if required for garnishing, use only two ounces of the gelatine for the same quantity of

other ingredients. By "liquid aspic jelly" is meant this jelly
before it is set.

All Moulds, etc, mentioned in the following pages are kept in stock, and can be had wholesale and retail at 32, Mortimer Street, W.

MOULDS FOR ICE PUDDINGS.

All Ice Moulds are made in reputed measure.

No. 1.—FRUIT TOP.   No. 2.—FLUTED TOP.

No. 3.—ROSE TOP.   No. 4.—STEP TOP.

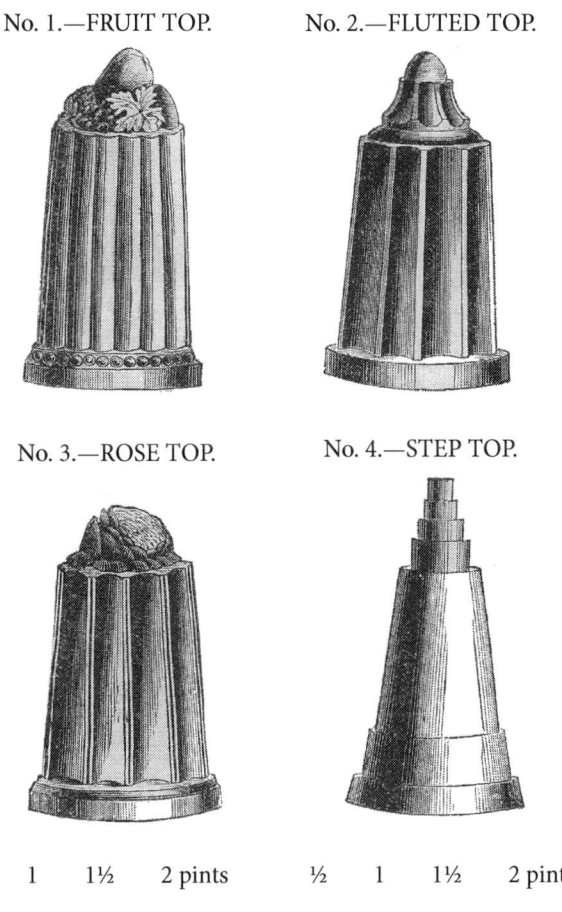

1   1½   2 pints   ½   1   1½   2 pints

PRICES ON APPLICATION.

No. 5.—FLUTED TOP.   No. 5.—FLUTED TOP.

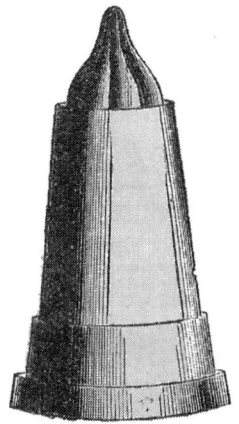   

No. 7.—WITH PLINTH.   No. 8.—WITH PLINTH.

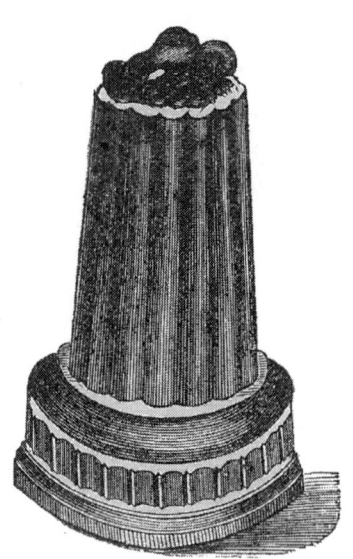   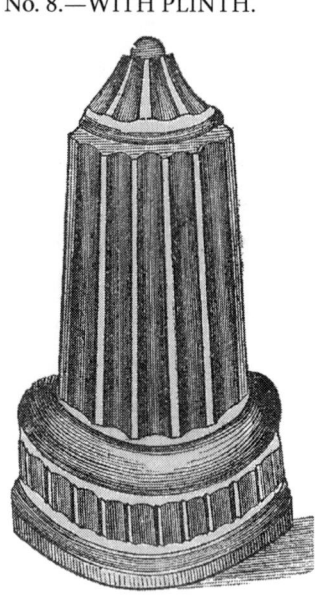

3 and 4 pints.   3 and 4 pints.

PRICES ON APPLICATION.

No. 10.—FLUTED TOP.

No. 8A.

VERY HANDSOME.

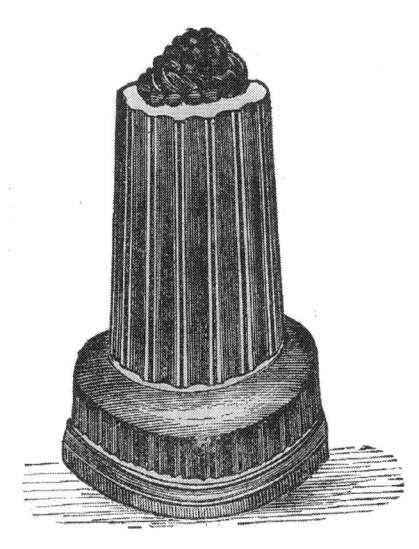

2 and 3 pints.

3 and 4 pints.

FANCY SHAPES.

No. 10A.—ICE TRAY.

No. 12.—GRAPE.

(Very bold and handsome.)

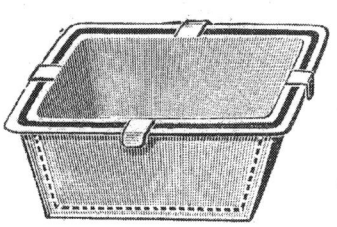

In tin, for Serving Sorbets, Fruit &c.

2½, 3 and 4 pints.

PRICES ON APPLICATION.

No. 13—ASPARAGUS.

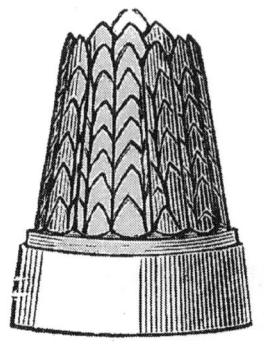

Height 5 inches, 1½ pints.

No. 14.—PLAIN MELON.

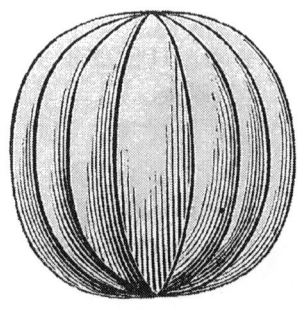

1½ pints.

No. 15.
SMALL BASKET.

Quart.

No.15A.
COUPE JACK MOULD.

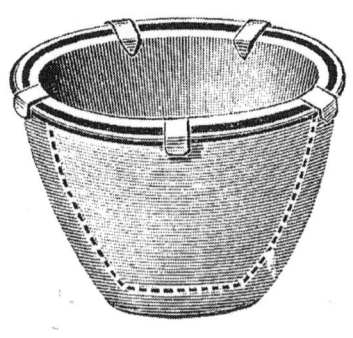

In tin, with lining.

PRICES ON APPLICATION.

No. 17.—OVAL MELON.

No. 14.
BASKET OF ROSES.

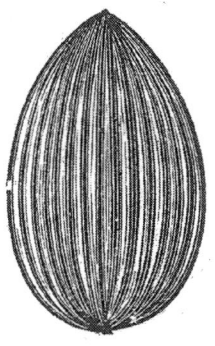

7 inches long, quart.

1 quart.

No. 36D.—BASKET OF CHERRIES.

No.20.—WHEATSHEAF.

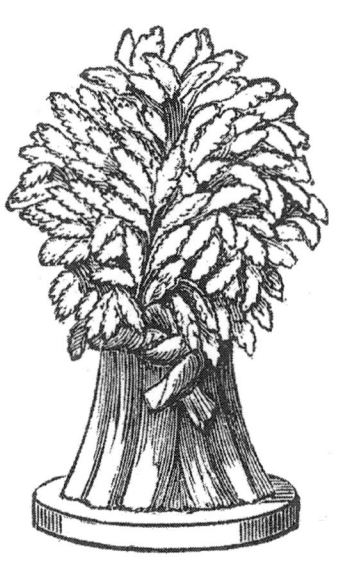

Very handsome.
3 pints.

8 inches high, 1 quart
3 pints.

PRICES ON APPLICATION.

No. 23E—COPPER.　　　　　　No. 29.—FISH.

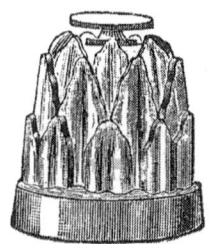

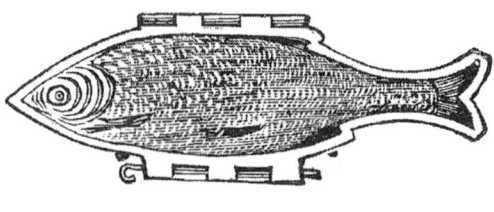

No. 30.—CUCUMBER.

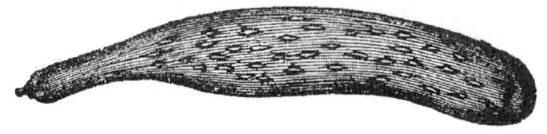

No. 31.—ASPARAGUS.

No. 32.—GARNISHING OR DESSERT ICE MOULDS.

Grapes, Lemon, Artichoke, Gherkin, Strawberry,
Peach, Plum, Pear, Currant, Corn, Orange, Apricot, Fish, Oyster,
Duck, Apple, and many others.

Peach.　Pine.　　Rose.　Basket of Grapes.　Pear.　Apple.
Cherries.

PRICES ON APPLICATION.

No. 33—TIN. No. 31.—ROSE TOP (PEWTER).

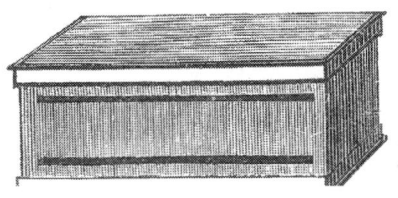

No. 1. No. 2.

No. 36—ICE PUDDING, SHOWING SHAPE PRODUCED.

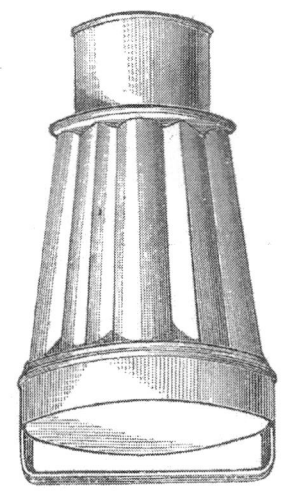 

No. 1 ... ... 1 pint.   No. 4 ... ... 3 pints.
No. 2 ... ... 1½ pint. No. 5 ... ... 4 pints
No. 3 ... ... 2 pint.

PRICES ON APPLICATION.

No. 42.—DUCK.

No. 43.—SWAN.

No. 45
BUNCH OF GRAPES.

No. 46
CAULIFLOWER.

No. 44
DOVE.

1¼ pints.

1 quart.

1 quart.

No. 47. —HEN.

No. 48. —FISH

1 quart.

1 quart.

No. 49.
PINEAPPLE.

No. 50. BASKET
OF FLOWERS.

No. 51.
PINEAPPLE.

1 quart.

1 quart.

1 quart and ½ pint.

PRICES ON APPLICATION.

No. 52.—BOMBE.   No. 36A.   No. 53.

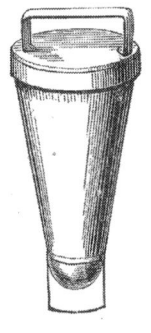

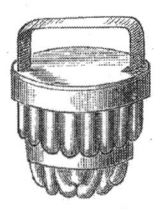

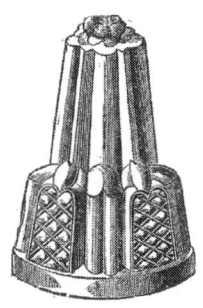

No. 1 ... 1 pint
No. 2 ... 1½ pints.

1 and 2 pints.   No. 3 ... 2 pints.   1 quart.

No. 55.—KOSIKI.   No. 56.   No. 57.—SUCCÈS.

1 quart.   1 quart.   1 quart.

No. 52.
No. 59.—BEEHIVE.   ICE WATER CUP.

No. 61.

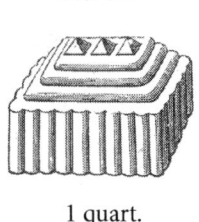

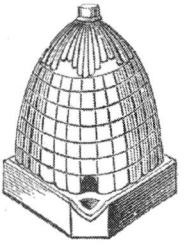

For making cups of
ice from water, etc.
For serving Sorbets,
Punch Romaine, etc.
In tinned copper.

1 quart.

1 quart.

PRICES ON APPLICATION.

FANCY MOULDS.
No. 52C.

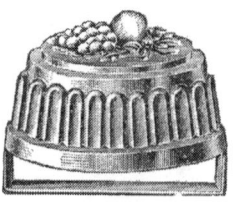

1 quart, and 5 pints.

No. 39D.	No. 39E	No. 39F.
		RABBIT. PEWTER

2 pints.	2 pints.	2 pints

No. 39G.	No. 39H.	No. 39r
FANCY MELON	FANCY	GIANT
PEWTER	BEEHIVE	STRAWBERRY
	PEWTER	PEWTER.

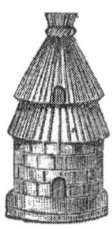

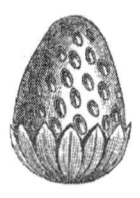

1, 1½ and 2 pints.	1 quart.	1 quart.

PRICES ON APPLICATION.

Necessaries for Sweet Making.

CARAMEL CUTTER.

To cut 20 squares ¾ in., 5/6 each.   To cut 30 squares ¾ in., 6/- each.
Any other size to order.

WOODEN SPATULAS.

Best Boxwood, 12 in., 1/- each.

SUGAR THERMOMETERS, 12/6 each.

CRYSTALLIZING TINS, with Sweet Fork, 12/6 each.

PALETTE KNIVES (Best English Make).

5,	6,	7,	8,	9,	10,
2/-	2/3	2/6	2/9	3/3	3/9

SUGAR SCRAPERS, 1/- each.

CORRUGATED RUBBER MOULDS, for Fondants.

12 moulds (4 each of 3 Patterns) in one plaque, 12/-
24   „   (4   „   6   „   )   „   22/-
48   „   (4   „   12   „   )   „   40/-

SUGAR DROPPERS, 7/- each.

TIN MOULDS for Chocolates, Fondants, Marzipan, 2/- per doz.
In plaques containing 6 moulds of one pattern, 5/- each.

Smaller Moulds of similar shapes, 1/6 per doz.

MARSHALL'S SCHOOL OF COOKERY.

BY ROYAL LETTERS PATENT.

MARSHALL'S PATENT FREEZER.

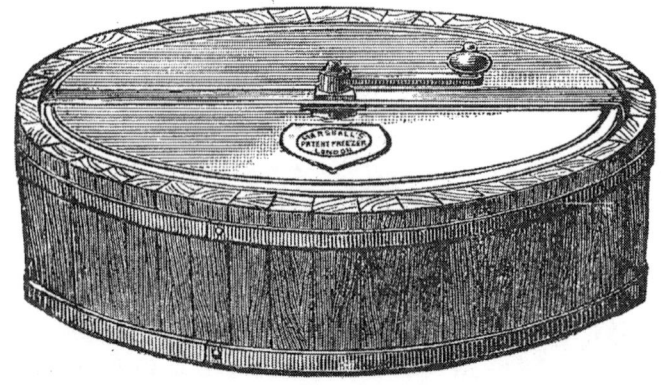

Complete view.

IS PRAISED BY ALL WHO KNOW IT FOR

CHEAPNESS in first cost.   CLEANLINESS in working.
ECONOMY in use.   SIMPLICITY in construction.
RAPIDITY in Freezing.

NO PACKING NECESSARY.   **NO SPATULA NECESSARY.**

Smooth and delicious Ice produced in 3 minutes.

SIZES—No. 1, to freeze any quantity up to one qt., £3.
No. 2, for two qts., £3 15.   No. 3, for four qts., £5 10.

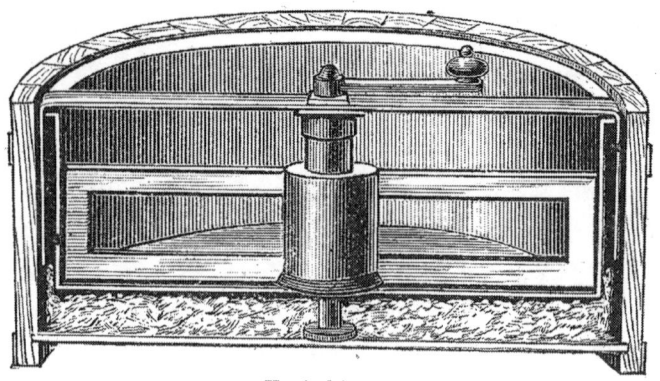

Vertical Section.

Showing the fan inside, which remains still while the pan revolves and scrapes up the film of ice as it forms on the bottom of the pan. The ice and salt is also shown *under* the pan; there is no need to pack any round the sides.

Can be ordered direct from MARSHALL'S SCHOOL OF COOKERY, or through any Ironmonger.

BY ROYAL LETTERS PATENT.

MARSHALL'S PATENT ICE CAVE.

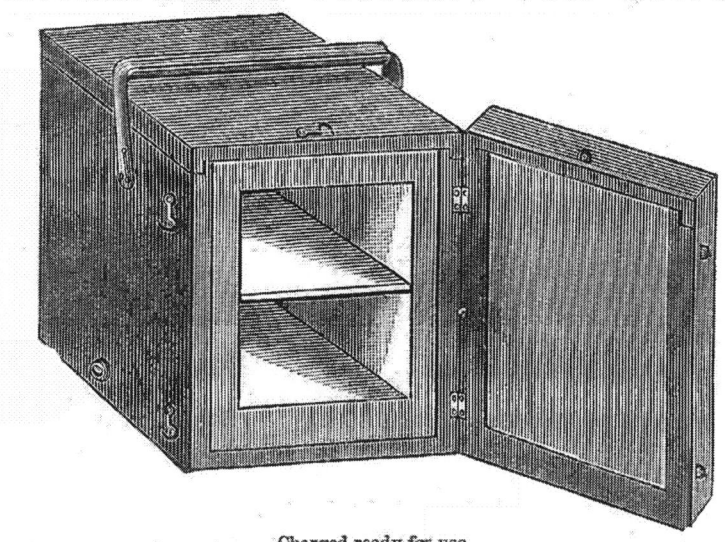

Charged ready for use.

USES.

FOR SETTING ICE PUDDINGS without the use of grease or chance of brine entering, and without the expense of special moulds. Ice puddings when moulded can be turned out and kept ready for use at any minute, so that the ice can be made and held ready before commencing to serve the dinner if necessary.

FOR FREEZING SOUFFLES it offers great advantages, as the progress of freezing can be examined from time to time. The souffés can always be kept ready for use.

FOR INVALIDS to have always at hand a supply of ice or iced food or drink, or for food or drink to be kept hot for any length of time. It is especially useful in nurseries, in the latter respect.

FOR CONFECTIONERS to send out ice puddings, etc., quite ready for serving; for keeping ice creams, etc., ready for selling.

FOR KEEPING ICES during Balls, Evening and Garden Parties, and for taking ice creams, etc., to Races, Picnics, etc.

AND FOR REFRIGERATORS GENERALLY.

SIZE 2, two quart moulds. Size 3, four quart moulds. Size 4 will hold six large champagne bottles. Sizes No. 2 and upwards can be used for icing mineral waters, etc., and kept in dining, smoking, and billiard rooms.

PRICES.

No. 2, £5 5s.   No. 3, £6 6s.   No. 3 Special, £6 6s.

No. 4, £7 7s.

Larger and special sizes to order.

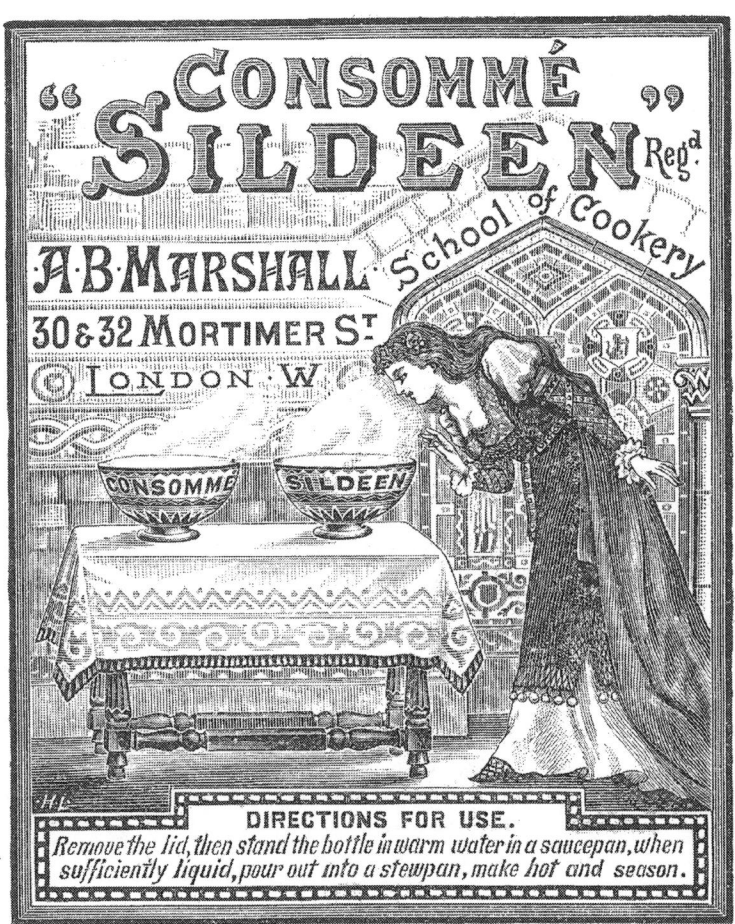

THIS IS THE LABEL (in colours).
Be sure you get it.

CONSOMMÉ SILDEEN

(REGISTERED)

Can now be procured of all leading Grocers, in
reputed Pint Bottles.

CONSOMMÉ SILDEEN. No house should be without a few
bottles of Consommé Sildeen in the store cupboard, ever ready to
welcome a guest or nourish an invalid.

A. B. MARSHALL, LTD., 32, Mortimer St., London, W.

Ask for "Marshall's" and see that you get it in the boxes as below.

THE PUREST, BEST, AND REALLY THE CHEAPEST.
Do not be put off with any other.

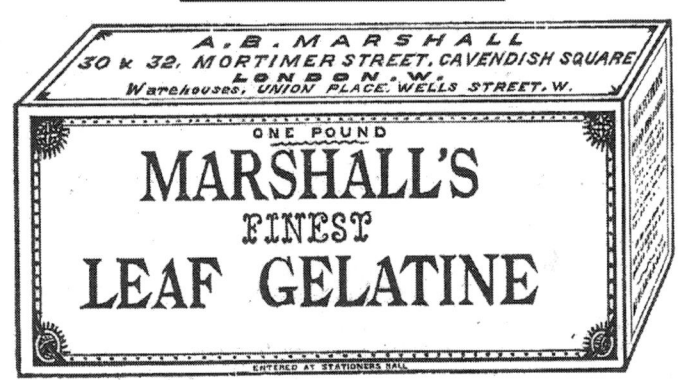

FOR DOMESTIC AND CULINARY PURPOSES.

 Sold only in White Cardboard Boxes, bearing Name and Address.

BEWARE OF UNWHOLESOME IMITATIONS.

MARSHALL'S FINEST LEAF GELATINE,

 Sold only in White Cardboard Boxes, with Name and Address, can in every respect be DEPENDED UPON.

MARSHALL'S FINEST LEAF GELATINE
STANDS UNRIVALLED FOR
QUALITY, STRENGTH, PURITY, DELICACY, AND CHEAPNESS.

MARSHALL'S SUPERFINE FELT JELLY BAGS.

Each drum contains a coupon, so many of which (see back of coupon) will be taken as payment for Mrs. A. B. Marshall's books, etc.

MARSHALL'S
HIGH-CLASS
BAKING POWDER.

This Registered Label is on every Drum.

STRENGTH as manufactured, exceeds 120 cubic inches of available gas for leavening purposes, per ounce of powder. Do not be put off with any other.

THE BEST QUALITY

MARSHALL'S BAKING POWDER

NONE GENUINE UNLESS SIGNED

A.B. Marshall

MADE WITH
INGREDIENTS OF THE FINEST QUALITY ONLY,
AND
STRENGTH. WEIGHT PURITY
ARE GUARANTEED
As stated on this Wrapper. See Analyst's Report.

The rights in the above Registered Label are the property of the Proprietors of
MARSHALL'S SCHOOL OF COOKERY,
32 & 30, MORTIMER STREET, LONDON. W.

GUARANTEE.—Every Grocer selling this Baking Powder is authorised to guarantee its purity, weight, and strength as stated. Ask for "Marshall's" and be sure you get it.

In Three Sizes, 1 lb., 10 oz., and 5 oz. drums.

ANALYTICAL REPORT BY CECIL H. CRIBB, B.Sc. (Lond.), F.I.C.,
Public Analyst to the Strand District, London, W.C.

LABORATORY, 136, SHAFTESBURY AVENUE,
LONDON, W., *Jan.* 16*th*, 1896.

MRS. A. B. MARSHALL.

DEAR MADAM,—I have made a complete analysis of the sample of Cowan's Baking Powder submitted to me, and find it to be composed of absolutely harmless ingredients, the gas-producing constituents being mixed in as nearly as possible theoretical proportions.

One ounce of the powder yields over 120 cubic inches of gas, which is evolved slowly and regularly.

It may in fact be considered an **ideal** one, having the maximum of **strength** consistent with **keeping qualities.**   Yours faithfully, (*Signed*) CECIL H. CRIBB.

A. B. Marshall's Selected Pure

CANE SUGAR

AS USED FOR

Sugar-Spinning, Boiling, etc.,

Is sold only in Packets containing 3 lbs. net.

(See Name and Address on every Packet.)

It is guaranteed free from Beetroot Sugar, Glucose, or Chemicals.

A. B. MARSHALL, LTD.,

32, Mortimer Street, Regent Street, London, W.

Warehouses : **Union Place, Wells Street, W.**

MARSHALL'S
(WHITE)
TARRAGON VINEGAR

This Tarragon Vinegar is prepared from freshly gathered Tarragon specially grown for the purpose, and represents the highest possible character of production.

This article is the choicest it is possible to produce under the most favourable circumstances, and the price is less than that often charged for the same quantity of other makes.

A trial is sure to give satisfaction.

Order of any Grocer, and see that the Label and Bottle bear the correct Name.

For the Programme of A. B. Marshall's Lessons,

as arranged for three weeks in advance, see

"THE TABLE"

Established 1886.

"**THE TABLE**" is published twice monthly, and may be had through any stationer, railway bookstall, or direct from "THE TABLE" Newspaper Company, 32, Mortimer Street, London, W., by Subscription, on terms as hereunder.

"**THE TABLE**" contains New Recipes by A. B. MARSHALL, and treats of Household and Table Decoration, the "Cuisine," Menus, Current Markets, Culinary Correspondence and Recipes, and Articles appertaining to Domestic and Household Affairs, and Food.

"**THE TABLE**" is greatly appreciated by all ladies interested in good cookery and other home matters, as shown by the long list of its subscribers, who are to be found in every centre of the Kingdom, and in the Colonies and United States, and it has a larger circulation than any other Paper devoted to similar objects.

"**THE TABLE**" is also taken by the leading Caterers and Hotel Proprietors in the Kingdom, by the Presidents of the Officers' Mess in Regiments at home and abroad, and by the largest Family Establishments throughout the country.

"**THE TABLE**" is larger and contains more matter than any of the Continental Journals devoted to the "Cuisine."

SUBSCRIPTIONS—PREPAID ONLY.

Post Free, One Year, 10s. 6d.   Six Months, 5s. 3d.

Single Copies 4d. each, by post 5d.

The Importance of Good Icing Sugar

IS KNOWN TO ALL

COOKS AND CONFECTIONERS.

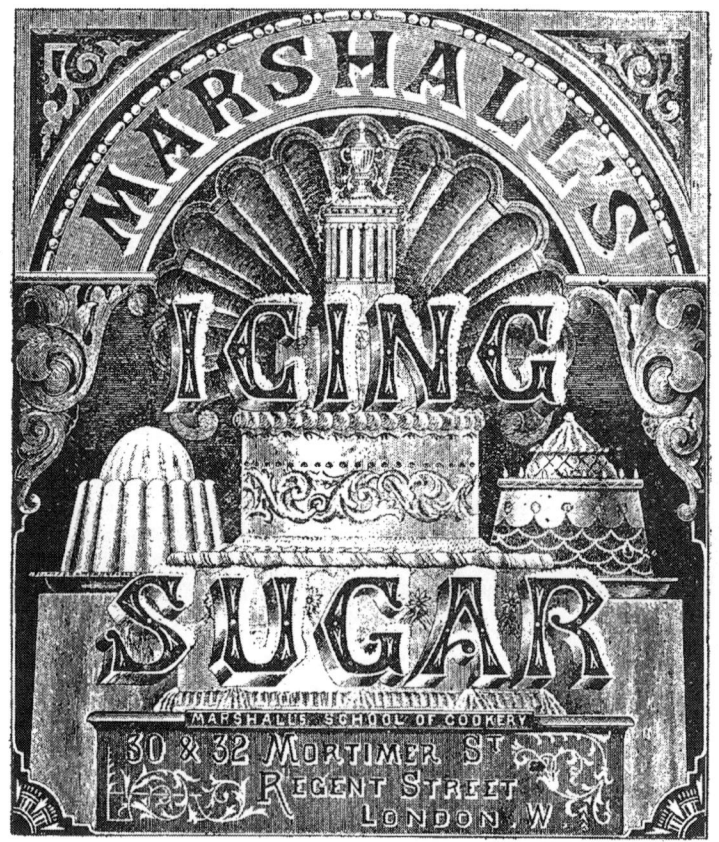

The above Registered Label is on all tins of

MARSHALL'S FINEST ICING SUGAR

Sold in 2 lb., 3 lb., and 7 lb. Tins.

INDEX

MOUSSES.

WATER ICES.

WATER AND PERFUMED ICES MADE FROM RIPE FRUITS, ETC.

Supplement to the

2022 Hardback Edition

GLOSSARY TO THE 2022 EDITION

This glossary, which is common both to The Book of Ices and Fancy Ices but was not included in the original editions, presents an explanation of contemporaneous ingredients and terms occurring in their original texts and, wherever possible, their modern equivalents. It may be impractical and even undesirable to adopt some methods cited in the original recipes. For example, the crushed cherry kernels, which may naturally contain small traces of cynanide, as an ingredient of Cherry Cream (page 13) and Cherry Water Ice (page 32), may be substituted by a half teaspoonful of almond extract, or by a teaspoonful of Amaretto liqueur.

alcohol The ingredients for many of A.B. Marshall's recipes include alcohol, such as white rum or a liqeuer. You should avoid the temptation to exceed the quantity specified in each case because alcohol inhibits freezing, so its overuse may result in a ice cream or other dish not fully freezing.

ballette mould A spherical mould divided into two around its circumference.

black-heart cherries Substitute any dark red variety.

cane sugar White granulated sugar made from sugar cane but sugar made from sugarbeet can be used instead.

Carolina rice Any pudding rice.

Catawba wine Substitute any good sweet or semi-sweet red wine.

cedrat A mild citrus fruit native to the Middle East. Grapefruit would make a good substitute.

coffee berries Coffee beans.

cornet tin A tapered tin mould to which the cornet mixture is adhered to the outside.

dish-paper A paper doiley.

en couronne In the shape of a crown or ring.

entremet A cake, originally served between courses, layered with mousse, jam, custard and other fillings.

filberts Hazelnuts

flour Although self-raising flour was invented by a Bristol baker in 1845, cereal plain flour should be used wherever flour is given as an ingredient.

foolscap paper A sheet of British Imperial paper measuring 8 inches x 13 inches (330mm x 203mm), so slightly narrower and longer than A4. Where a recipe specifies its use, such as a supporting collar for a soufflé, use baking or parchment paper.

Fry's Caracas Chocolate Substitute the same quantity of 70%

plain chocolate.

Fry's Chocolate Varieties Any good-quality chocolate assortment.

Fry's Powdered Caracas Chocolate Substitute the same quantity of drinking chocolate powder.

Fry's Powdered Vanilla Chocolate Substitute the same quantity of drinking chocolate powder.

Fry's Pure Concentrated Cocoa Substitute any brand of cocoa powder.

Fry's Vanilla Chocolate Substitute any brand of milk chocolate.

George's Cheltenham Wafers No record could be found of this Victorian product but it may have been a thin light biscuit like the modern wafer.

ginger brandy A liqueur made from brandy infused with ginger, vanilla, orange zest and sugar

hair sieve Use a fine metal or plastic sieve

half-peach mould Exactly as it seems. Period examples in copper are often available online – as are modern silicone equivalents, but make sure they are suitable for culinary use.

ice cave, cave A metal-lined wooden box packed with ice and coarse salt that performed the storage function of the modern freezer.

Jordan almonds Any almonds, shelled and skin removed.

Liebig Company's extract of meat Substitute an appropriate quantity of beef stock granules.

loaf sugar Substitute sugar cubes.

macédoine An assortment of finely chopped vegetables or fruits served raw or cooked, hot or cold.

Maidenhair Fern A house plant having a delicate lacy foliage, available from garden centres and online.

Marshall's Apricot Yellow Substitute any light-to-moderate yellow food colouring, preferably natural.

Marshall's Carmine [E120 Cochineal] Most but necessarily not all natural food colourings are derived from plants. The known exception is natural red food colouring, derived from crushed cactus insects. Not all synthetic food colourings are suitable for vegans but many vegan-friendly brands of food colourings are available in the UK and USA. Brands include Lakeland and Sugarflair.

Marshall's Cherry Red Substitute a natural food colouring of that colour.

Marshall's Coffee Brown Substitute a natural food colouring of that colour.

Marshall's Coralline A pepper made from a reddish seaweed. Substitute sweet paprika powder or mild cayenne powder.

Marshall's Damson Blue Substitute a natural food colouring of that colour.

Marshall's Leaf Gelatine Use any modern brand of leaf gelatine or the equivalent standard or vegetarian gelatine granules.

Marshall's Sap Green A medium-green food colouring based on a medieval artist's paint made from ripe buckthorn berries. Substitute another natural food colouring of the same colour.

Marshall's Vanilla Essence Substitute natural vanilla extract or vanilla paste.

new milk Fresh whole milk, not semi-skimmed or skimmed milk, should always be used for making ice creams and other desserts.

Moscovite currants Redcurrants

Neopolitan mould A rectangular tin or pewter mould usually divided into three horizontally, to permit the presentation of layered ice creams having different flavours or colours.

Noyeau liqeuer/syrup An almond-flavoured liqueur (now named Noyau or Crème de Noyaux) made from apricot or cherry kernels or cherry pits. Substitute Amaretto liqueur.

orange flower water Orange juice or a diluted triple-sec orange liqueur may be substituted.

pineapple essence Use a natural essence or extract product.

plombière A desert made of ice cream and glacé fruits.

quart A liquid measure equivalent to 2 pints, 40 fluid ounces or a little under one litre.

Rahat Lakoum Turkish Delight

ratafias Almond biscuits

red gooseberries Sweeter than the green variety but not widely available unless you grow your own. Substitute green gooseberries and increase the amount of sugar specified in the recipe to taste.

St. Julien Use any good claret (Bordeaux).

saccharometer   A glass, plastic or electronic device for measuring sugar density in a liquid, sold by retailers of home brewing equipment.

saltspoonful Equivalent to one quarter of a teaspoonful; a good pinch.

sealing wax When stated as a means of securing paper collars, etc, substitute cook's twine, aka butcher's string.

soluble cocoa Cocoa powder, not drinking chocolate.

Spanish nuts Tigernuts. They are actually a tuber, so the peeled product is claimed not to pose a threat to those with a nut allergy.

Succès A type of mould. See page 67.

tammy cloth, tammy A course woollen material once used for straining liquids. Use instead a fine-mesh metal or plastic strainer.

threepenny piece A British low-value, pre-decimal coin. The late Victorian minting had approximately the same surface area as a today's 5p coin or American dime.

Tokay Hungarian sweet white wine. Marsala or Muscat may be used instead.

uncrystallised cherries Fresh cherries.

vanilla essence Use instead an equivalent measure of natural vanilla extract or paste.

whipping pan, whipping tin Use a large plastic or metal mixing bowl.

white-heart cherry A variety having a cream-coloured flesh with blushes of pale red.

white wax Used in baking by Victorian and later cooks for its non-stick properties. Substitute non-stick foil or baking parchment.

MODERN EQUIPMENT
AND METHODS FOR MAKING
FROZEN DESSERTS

WHEN Agnes Bertha Marshall published *The Book of Ices* and her later, more extensive *Fancy Ices* collection in the 1890s, professional chefs and cooks (including even those working in grand houses and stately homes) all had to rely on a wooden churn packed with rock ice and salt, such as that illustrated on page XX, to produce frozen desserts.

Today's home cook can choose from several electric ice cream makers or accessories capable of producing the fully frozen, ready-to-eat dish in under an hour.

The home cook's simplest and least expensive option uses a metal bowl containing coolant trapped within its double walls that is first placed empty in a freezer, because few refrigerators have an ice box large enough, for at least eight hours ahead of preparing the ingredients to be frozen. The bowl typically holds 1 to 1½ litres (1¾ to 3½ pints) of mixture but room should be allowed for expansion as the motorised

paddle introduces more and more air during churning.

The bowl is then inserted into the body of the appliance (*an example of this type is shown above*) and the lid housing the detachable motor and paddle assembly is fitted. When the motor is started and the paddle begins turning, the prepared mixture is added through a chute in the lid and is left churning for the recommended time given in the instruction manual. The resulting dessert can either be eaten immediately or the bowl returned to the freezer until the dish is to be served.

The disadvantage of this type of equipment is that planning ahead is required, though it usually possible to purchase a spare bowl that can be kept in the freezer ready for use whenever required.

The detachable motor unit of such appliances should never be immersed in water for cleaning, and it is likely that none of the of the other components will be dishwasher safe.

If you already own a KitchenAid or Kenwood stand mixer, an equally affordable option is the attachment available for most models. Again, it takes the form of a coolant-lined bowl that has to be pre-frozen (KitchenAid recommend for 15 hours or overnight) and paddle.

The KitchenAid attachment (*pictured below*) is compatible with all the brand's current and older stand mixers, with the exception of the 3.3 L model.

The Kenwood bowl-and-paddle attachment is used in a similar way. Different versions are available for the Chef, Chef XL, kMix, Cooking Chef and Sense models.

The most sophisticated and expensive home appliance for making frozen desserts is the Sage Smart Scoop, which

incorporates its own onboard compressor, so pre-freezing of the removable bowl is not required.

The Smart Scoop (*pictured above*) even has an optional bowl-chill function, which makes for smaller ice crystals in the finished dessert, to give a smoother consistency. The digital control panel has presets for sorbet, frozen yoghurt, gelato and ice cream, and offers soft-to-hard adjustment of each type. The optional keep-cool function operates the compressor intermittently when the chosen programame ends, to prevent the dessert from melting for up to three hours.

Most of the preparation terms used by Agnes Bertha Marshall will be familiar to today's home cook, with a few exceptions. For example, fine chopping can be done using a stand-alone grinder or food processor, and pureé can be produced in a food processor. Other substitutes are offered in the Glossary to this edition (pages 97-103).

Printed in Great Britain
by Amazon

54aad5f4-1461-4272-90e5-f1004d518f76R01